MW00880512

...mer marketing
...mer termination
...other customer costs
...er profit by segment
...ing

$105,000.00
$150,000.00
$80,000.00
$335,000.00
($35,000.00)
0%

Metrics:

...ost per acquired customer
...st per terminated customer
...keting cost per active customer

[Segment Name]

$52,500.00

TABLE OF CONTENT

INTRODUCTION   12

BOOK 1:
_____

WHAT IS MICROSOFT EXCEL?   15

    1.1 OPENING MICROSOFT EXCEL   18
    1.2 GO TO MY COMPUTER AND OPEN IT   19
    1.3 OPEN THE MICROSOFT OFFICE FOLDER FROM THE   19
    1.4 FEATURES OF MS EXCEL   19
    1.4.1 Cell   19
    1.4.2 A work or spreadsheet   19
    1.4.3 Worksheet   20
    1.4.4 Workbook   20
    1.4.5 Excel's Graphical Design   21
    1.4.6 Excel's Database Functionality   21
    1.4.7 Excel Tools & Functions   21
    1.4.8 Home   21
    1.4.9 Insert   21
    1.4.10 Page Layout   22
    1.4.11 Formulas   22

BOOK 2:
_____

UNDERSTANDING & GETTING STARTED WITH MICROSOFT EXCEL   31

    2.1 WHAT IS THE BEST WAY TO USE MICROSOFT EXCEL?   33
    2.1.1 Open a New Workbook   33
    2.1.2 Including a Worksheet   33
    2.1.3 Changing the Name of a Worksheet   33
    2.1.4 Use the Ribbon in Excel   34
    2.1.5 Ribbon Tabs   35
    2.1.6 Ribbon Bar   35
    2.1.7 Using Worksheets to Manage Data   35

BOOK 3:

FORMULAS & FUNCTIONS OF THE MICROSOFT EXCEL   49

3.1 USES IN FINANCE AND ACCOUNTING	50
3.2 BASIC TERMS IN EXCEL	51
3.2.1 Formulas	51
3.2.2 Functions	51
3.3 HOW TO USE FUNCTIONS & FORMULAS	52
3.3.1 Make Changes to the Formula	53
3.4 BASIC EXCEL FORMULAS	54
3.5 SUM	54
3.6 SUBTRACTION	55
3.7 DIVISION	56
3.8 MULTIPLICATION	57
3.9 PERCENTAGE	57
3.10 RANDOM NUMBERS GENERATOR	59
3.11 TIPS FOR USING FUNCTION CORRECTLY	59
3.11.1 Insertion of Function	59
3.11.2 Remove the Formula but Keep the Result	62
3.11.3 Operator Precedence	62
3.11.4 Do Not Use Dual Quotes to Enclose Amounts	63
3.11.5 Copy/Paste the Formula	64
3.11.6 In Excel formulas, do not format numbers	66
3.11.7 Check that Calculation Options is set to Automatic	**67**

BOOK 4:

MS EXCEL TEXT'S FUNCTIONS   69

4.1 CONCATENATE	70
4.2 LEFT, MID, & RIGHT	71
4.2.1 LEFT	71
4.2.2 MID	72
4.2.3 RIGHT	73
4.3 TRIM	74
4.4 LEN	75
4.5 PROPER	76
4.6 SEARCH FUNCTION	76
4.7 TEXTJOIN FUNCTION	78
4.8 LOWER FUNCTION	80
4.9 UPPER FUNCTION	81

BOOK 5

MS EXCEL LOGIC'S FUNCTIONS

5.1 AND & OR   84
5.2 IF   84
5.3 MAX & MIN   85
5.4 EVEN & ODD   88
5.5 IFS FUNCTION   88
5.5.1 Rating from Highest to Lowest   89
5.6 NOT FUNCTION   90

BOOK 6

MS EXCEL COUNTING FUNCTIONS

6.1 COUNT   94
6.2 COUNTA   95
6.3 COUNTBLANK   95
6.4 COUNTIF   97

BOOK 7

CONDITIONAL FUNCTIONS IN MS EXCEL

7.1 AVERAGE   100
7.2 COUNTIFS   100
7.3 SUMIFS FUNCTION   102
7.4 MINIFS FUNCTION   103
7.5 AVERAGEIF   104
7.6 AVERAGEIFS   105

BOOK 8

MS EXCEL FUNCTIONS OF DATE & TIME

8.1 TODAY & NOW   108
8.2 END OF MONTH   108
8.3 DATEDIF   109
8.4 WORKDAY FUNCTION   110
8.5 NETWORKDAYS   111

8.6 DATE FUNCTION 112
8.7 EDATE FUNCTION 113
8.8 WEEKDAY FUNCTION 114

BOOK 9

EXCEL PROBLEMS & THEIR SOLUTIONS 117

9.1 COPY THE FORMULA 118
9.2 FILL IN THE CELLS RAPIDLY 118
9.2.1 Total a Row or a Column 119
9.2.2 Delete Double Rows 119
9.3 CHOOSE TO REMOVE DUPLICATES KEY 119
9.3.1 Filters 119
9.3.2 Copy the Values 119
9.4 IMPORT A TABLE FROM THE INTERNET 120
9.5 FAST AGGREGATION 121
9.6 IFERROR 122
9.7 IFNA 123
9.8 FORMULAS NOT WORKING 124
9.9 FORMULA VIEW 125
9.10 HASHES IN THE CELL 125
9.11 PAGE BREAKS 126
9.12 EXCEL SECURITY 126

BOOK 10

PIVOT TABLE IN MS EXCEL 129

10.1 WHY ARE PIVOT TABLES IMPORTANT? 130
10.2 CREATING PIVOT TABLES 131
10.2.1 Drag Fields 132
10.2.2 Sorting 134
10.3 PRACTICAL EXAMPLES OF A PIVOT TABLE 135
10.4 SORTING DATA BY A SPECIFIC TRAIT 138
10.5 DRAG & DROP A FIELD IN THE AREA OF "ROW LABELS" 138
10.6 FINE-TUNE THE CALCULATIONS 140
10.7 FILTERING 140
10.8 CHANGE SUMMARY CALCULATION 141
10.9 TWO-DIMENSIONAL PIVOT TABLE 143
10.9.1 New AI Features in Excel 145
10.10 MACROS 146

BOOK 11

CHARTS & GRAPHS WITH MICROSOFT EXCEL   147

11.1 ONE MUST THINK IS CHART AND GRAPH ARE THE SAME THINGS? 148
11.2 CHARTS IN EXCEL   149
11.3 TYPES OF CHARTS   150
11.3.1 Pie charts   151
11.3.2 Doughnut Chart   151
11.3.3 Bar Chart   152
11.3.4 Line Chart   154
11.3.5 Combo Chart   154
11.3.6 Stock Chart   155
11.3.7 Bubbles Chart   155
11.3.8 Area Chart   155
11.3.9 Surface Chart   156
11.3.10 Importance of Charts   156
11.4 GRAPHS IN EXCEL   157
11.5 TYPES OF GRAPHS IN EXCEL   158
11.5.1 Line Graph   158
11.5.2 Column Graphs   158
11.5.3 Bar Graphs   159
11.6 CREATING GRAPHS & CHARTS IN EXCEL   159
11.6.1 Layout   163
11.6.2 Format   164
11.7 CREATING CHARTS WITH MS EXCEL   165
11.7.1 Select the Desired Subtype by Clicking on It   166
11.7.2 Change the Chart's Style   167
11.7.3 Row/Column Switching   169
11.7.4 Labels for Data   171
11.8 CREATING TABLE IN EXCEL   172

BOOK 12

BENEFITS & APPLICATIONS OF MICROSOFT EXCEL   175

12.1 APPLICATIONS OF MICROSOFT EXCEL   176
12.1.1 Data Analysis and Storage   176
12.1.2 Excel's Applications Help One to Do the Job
Faster and More Efficiently   176
12.1.3 Spreadsheets & Data Recovery
                                    176

12.1.4 MS Excel's Mathematical Calculations Make the
Calculation Simpler 177
12.1.5 Security 177
12.1.6 Get Data Displays More Sophisticatedly 177
12.1.7 Online Access 178
12.1.8 Keeps All of the Data in One Place 178
12.1.9 Assists Businesspeople in Implementing Long-Term Strategies 178
12.1.10 Manage Expenses 179
12.2 BUSINESS USES FOR MICROSOFT EXCEL 179
12.2.1 MS Excel has the ability to store and interpret
vast amounts of data 179
12.2.2 Business Data Collection & Verification 180
12.2.3 Administrative & Management Responsibilities 180
12.2.4 Budgeting & Accounting 180
12.2.5 Examine the Data 181
12.2.6 Visualizations and Reporting 181
12.2.7 Assumption 181
12.3 BENEFITS OF USING MS EXCEL 182
12.3.1 Accounting 182
12.3.2 Graphing 182
12.3.3 Inventory Management 182
12.3.4 Schedules & Calendars 182
12.3.5 Seating Tables 183
12.3.6 Worksheet for Goal Setting 183
12.3.7 Mock-Ups 183
12.3.8 Complete Your Tasks 183
12.3.9 Task List 183
12.3.10 Item Lists 184
12.3.11 Schematics for Project Management 184
12.3.12 Timesheets 184
12.3.13 Types of Documents 184
12.3.14 Quizzes 185
12.3.15 Keeping in Touch 186
12.3.16 CRM 186
12.3.17 E-Mail List 186
12.3.18 It's All for Entertainment 187
12.3.19 Logbooks from the Past 187
12.3.20 Sudoku 188
12.3.21 Words Clouds 188
12.3.22 Data Storage 188
12.4 MICROSOFT EXCEL: POINTS TO REMEMBER 189

BOOK 13

TIPS, SHORTCUTS & TECHNIQUES
FOR MICROSOFT EXCEL $\quad$ 191

13.1 WHY USE EXCEL SHORTCUTS? $\quad$ 192
13.1.1 Excel Basics' Shortcuts $\quad$ 192
13.2 SHORTCUTS FOR THE MICROSOFT EXCEL $\quad$ 193
13.3 KEYBOARD SHORTCUTS $\quad$ 196
13.4 TIPS & TECHNIQUES $\quad$ 197
13.4.1 Matching Indexes $\quad$ 197
13.4.2 Increase the Number of Leading Zeros $\quad$ 197
13.4.3 Repeat Header for Printing $\quad$ 198
13.4.4 Name the Ranges $\quad$ 198
13.4.5 Finding a Linked Value $\quad$ 198
13.4.6 Converting Numbers to Ranges $\quad$ 200
13.4.7 Text to Column $\quad$ 201
13.4.8 Excel should be taught not to jump to outcomes. $\quad$ 201
13.4.9 Format just a portion of the cell $\quad$ 202
13.4.10 In Excel, insert credit card numbers $\quad$ 202

Conclusion $\quad$ **203**

EXCEL VIDEO TUTORIALS LINK ON PAGE 191

INTRODUCTION

Microsoft Excel is a spreadsheet program that was created and released by the company Microsoft. It was included in the Microsoft Office productivity suite. Excel assembles data in rows and columns but unlike Microsoft Word. The intersection of row & column is called a cell. A single piece of data, like text, an expected value, or a formula, may be entered into every cell. During creation, Excel was given the alias Odyssey. On September 30 in 1985, it was first published. Spreadsheets (Worksheets) are created in MS Excel to store and arrange data in a tabular form. MS Excel is among the most widely distributed software program worldwide.

Excel has effective functions and tools, and it is used in a broad range of applications by multinational Information Technology companies. Data entry, reading, and simulation are all easy. Excel organizes the data into effective forms; working on it is easier. Spreadsheets are created in MS Excel to any arranged data. Excel is commonly used for data organization and financial reporting. It is seen in both corporate functions and for businesses of all sizes.

MS Excel is compatible with nearly any other element of Office software. Excel worksheets can be quickly applied to Word files or PowerPoint presentations to make them more visually complex.

- Data entry
- Charting & graphing
- Data management
- Financial analysis
- Time management
- Programming
- Financial modeling
- Accounting
- Task management
- Customer relationship administration
- Anything that has to be organized

In reality, many businesses depend solely on Excel worksheets for their financial planning, planning, and accounting needs. Although Excel is an "information" processing method, the most popular data that is handled is financial data. Although several bits of financial software are designed to execute complex functions, Excel's resiliency and accessibility are its best features.

Excel templates should be as efficient as the analyst wants.

All-new 2016 apps
Shop on MicrosoftStore.com
www.office.com
with the onli
Excel
Calen
Explore Offic

BOOK 1
What Is Microsoft Excel?

Microsoft has produced various products over the years, ranging from the Windows operating system and workplace management software and Xbox game consoles and much more. However, one product sticks out as the most adopted market program and has since become a standard in several businesses. MS Excel is database software that was first launched in 1985 to assist businesses in their financial management. In 2019, it evolved into a worldwide norm for everything, including the management of company records. As per Microsoft CEO, Excel is one of the finest consumer products the company has ever created and reflects the company's values. MS Excel includes various resources for performing tasks such as estimates, pivot tables, graphing tools, macro programming, and more. It works for various operating systems, including Windows, Mac, iOS, macOS & Android. A table is created by a series of columns & rows in an Excel work or spreadsheet. Columns usually are allocated alphabetically, while rows are typically assigned numbers. A cell is the intersection of columns and rows. A cell's address is determined by the letter representing the column and the no. representing the row.

For data processing and reporting, Microsoft Excel is a useful and efficient application. It's a spreadsheet program with multiple columns & rows; each cell contains a piece of single data information or material.

You will consider details easy to locate and instantly draw information from evolving data by grouping the data in this manner.

Microsoft Excel is used by everyone from the accounting firm to the receptionist, HR to the admin department. It is not exclusive to big corporations; small business owners and college students use it daily. There is something one does not overlook. Learning simple Excel tasks is a must at this age if you want to get a career. It has been in use over the last thirty years, and it has been updated with new updates during that period.

Excel's greatest advantage is that it can be used for a wide range of company activities, like statistics, economics, data collection, planning, reporting, product and billing tracking, and data analytics.

BELOW ARE SOME OF THE ITEMS
IT WILL DO FOR ONESELF:

Templates / Dashboards

Number calculating

Automation of Tasks

Import & store Data

Manipulating Text

Charts & Graphs

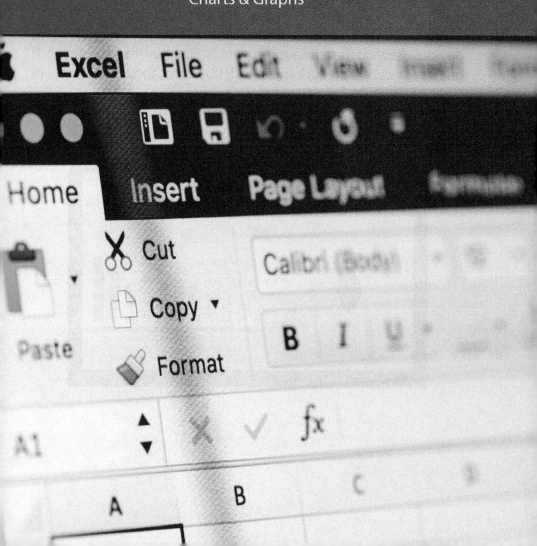

1.1 OPENING MICROSOFT EXCEL

Follow the instructions below to open Microsoft Excel on the computer:

- Go to Start
- Click All Programs
- Search MS office and choose it
- Select the Microsoft Excel option

Put another way, and one should use the Start button to look for Microsoft Excel in the open search box.

Excel can be found in the Start menu whether one has Excel or the whole Microsoft Office kit loaded on the computer.

Bear in mind that Excel is not used on modern computers. Before one can use it on the computer, one must first buy it and update it. If one does not want to (or can't afford) buy Excel, they can download a free trial edition from the Microsoft Office site.

If one has Excel loaded but it isn't showing up in the Start menu, use the measures below to manually activate it.

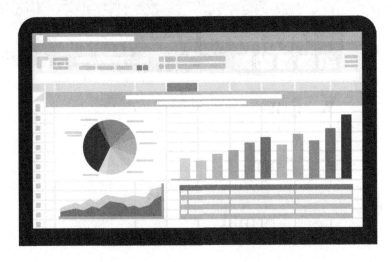

1.2 GO TO MY COMPUTER AND OPEN IT

Pick the C: by clicking or selecting it. If you have Microsoft Office loaded on the drive other than C: use that drive, then.

1.3 Open the Microsoft Office Folder from the Program Files Folder If there is a default folder in Microsoft Office, open it. And open the OfficeXX archive, the Office edition set up on one's device (for example, Office16 is for MS Office 2016). If one doesn't see a root folder, search for and access a folder called "Office."
Locate a file called EXCEL.EXE and click it to launch the Excel software.

1.4 FEATURES OF MS EXCEL

The below are the three most critical elements of Excel that one should learn first:

1.4.1 CELL

It is the spreadsheet's smallest yet most important component in the cell. One has the option of typing or copy-pasting the data into the cell. A text, a date, or a number may all be considered data. One may also alter its scale, font color, background color, borders, and other features. Per cell is known by its cell address, which includes the column and row numbers.

1.4.2 A WORK OR SPREADSHEET

It is a table with rows and columns of information. A cell is a rectangular box formed by the collision of rows and columns. An example of a cell is seen below:

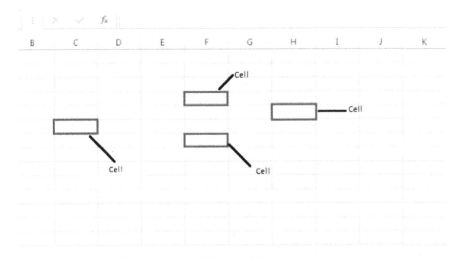

1.4.3 WORKSHEET

Each worksheet consists of independent cells and may contain text, or a formula, or a value. It also has a drawing layer that contains charts, pictures, and diagrams but is not visible. By pressing the button at the lower part of the workbook window, one can reach each spreadsheet in the workbook. A workbook may also store chart sheets, which show a simple chart and are accessed by clicking a button.

1.4.4 WORKBOOK

This, like every other program, is a different file. There are one or two worksheets in every workbook. A workbook may also refer to a series of several worksheets or one worksheet. One may add or remove worksheets, hide them without removing them, and rearrange the order in which they appear in the workbook.

An Excel spreadsheet can be edited and formatted in a variety of ways. The different features of Microsoft Excel are described below.

Excel's characteristics that make it the most commonly used techniques are as follows:

1.4.5 EXCEL'S GRAPHICAL DESIGN

Excel has a wide range of interactive features for representing data in graphs. Charts, Shapes, Clip Arts, Pictures, & Smart Arts, for instance.

1.4.6 EXCEL'S DATABASE FUNCTIONALITY

Excel may be used as a database and for a variety of data processing tasks. Slicers, Tables, Filtering, Sparklines, Pivot Tables, Database, Filtering, Data Validation, Sorting, Grouping, among other features, are examples.

1.4.7 EXCEL TOOLS & FUNCTIONS

They can assist you in performing efficient calculations and enhancing the Application Features. Formulas, VBA Macros, Hyperlinks, Add-ins, Spell Check, Security, and Conditional Formatting, so on are examples.

The layout of features in MS Excel is seen in the picture below:

1.4.8 HOME

The home part of the MS Excel consists of Font size, font color, font types, color for background, color palette, spacing, formatting choices and styles, cell addition and deletion, and editing options are also included.

1.4.9 INSERT

Table shape and type, incorporating photos and numbers, header and footer choices, adding tables, maps, sparklines, equation, formula, and symbol options are included in the insert portion.

1.4.10 PAGE LAYOUT

The page layout choice includes choices for themes, alignment, and page configuration.

1.4.11 FORMULAS

Since MS Excel can generate tables with a vast volume of details, one can use this function to apply formulas to the table and get faster results.

1.4.12 DATA

This group includes features such as adding additional data (from the internet), search options, and data resources.

1.4.13 REVIEW

In the analysis category, checking (such as spell check) can be performed on an excel document, and a user can add notes in this section.

1.4.14 VIEW

Here is where one can adjust the views under which the spreadsheet is viewed. This segment contains options for zooming in and out as well as pane layout.

1.4.15 SHORTCUT MENU

The shortcut menu allows one to navigate the most often used Excel commands and features easily. To use this function, right-click or the item one wants to edit on a Laptop, or control-click the element one wants to edit on a Mac. Based on the feature you've chosen, the choices shown will change.

4.16 BASICS IN SPREADSHEETS

Every Excel file is a workbook of several worksheets. The worksheet consists of a series of columns (denoted by letters) and rows (denoted by figures). The blue buttons from the top of the worksheet represent the letters of the columns. The row numbers are shown by the blue buttons on the spreadsheet's left hand. A cell is a point where a column and a row meet. One may fill in the blanks with your details. Text, figures, and formulas for automated calculations may all be entered into cells. The cell address for every cell on the worksheet is the column letter preceded by the row number.

1.4.17 FORMULA BAR

When one uses Excel, the formula bar would be one of the most important features. The formula bar displays all of the information and procedures that were used to restore the contents of a cell. When one enters data into a cell, the performance, or final outcome, is shown when moving the cursor away from the cell. This is particularly noticeable when utilizing functions since one just sees the outcome of the equation in the cell in the spreadsheet, not the entire equation. The formula bar is underneath the ribbon, which takes up the majority of the window.

While hiding the formula bar is feasible, and it is not advised. Select Excel Options at the right (bottom) of the menu that appears when one presses the Office button to remove or reveal the formula bar if it has been obscured by error. To see the formula bar, select the 'Advanced' option and tick the box for the Display formula bar underneath Display. Simply press Ok when you're done.

1.4.18 HEADER & FOOTER

One can have a header and a footer in their spreadsheet.

1.4.19 "FIND & REPLACE" FUNCTION

Microsoft Excel enables one to locate required data (numbers, texts) inside a spreadsheet and to substitute old data with new information.

1.4.20 PASSWORD PROTECTION

It helps the consumer to shield their spreadsheets from unwanted entry by encrypting them with a password.

1.4.21 DATA FILTERING

It is a fast and simple way to locate and manipulate a piece of data in a set only the rows that follow the criterion one applies for a column appear in a filtered range.

For sorting ranges in Excel, there are two commands:

- **AutoFilter:** This provides a selection-based filter with basic parameters.
- **Advanced Filter:** It uses parameters that are more complicated.

1.4.22 SORTING DATA

The method of organizing data into a logical order is known as data sorting. One can sort data in descending or ascending order in Excel.

1.4.23 FORMULAS THAT ARE BUILT-IN

Microsoft Excel has several built-in formulas for sums, averages, and minimums, among other things. One may use such formulae as per their needs.

1.4.24 MAKE VARIOUS GRAPHS (PIVOT TABLE)

Microsoft Excel helps one to make various charts like a bar graph, line diagrams, & pie- charts, etc.

1.4.25 INSTANTLY EDIT THE RESULT

Microsoft Excel immediately edits the outcome if any modifications are made in any of the cells.

1.4.26 AUDITING FORMULAS

Use formula auditing, and one may graphically represent or map the interactions between cells, formulas with blue arrows. One may track the precedents, or the dependents allows you to interpret and compare results quickly.

Some shortcuts for windows and Mac.

Action	Windows	Mac
Select active cell only	Shift Backspace	⇧ Delete
Show the active cell on worksheet	Ctrl Backspace	⌘ Delete
Move active cell clockwise in selection	Ctrl .	^ .
Move active cell down in selection	Enter	Return
Move active cell up in selection	Shift Enter	⇧ Return
Move active cell right in a selection	Tab	Tab
Move active cell left in a selection	Shift Tab	⇧ Tab

1.5 HISTORY OF THE MICROSOFT EXCEL

Dan Bricking, a Harvard Business School researcher, developed the VisiCalc software in 1978. It was a small application with just a few minimal features. It could only work for data in a matrix with five columns and twenty rows.

Bob Frankston, the co-founder of VisiCalc, was employed by Bricking to turn VisiCalc more efficiently. Frankston improved the program's pace and mathematics.

VisiCalc was an immediate hit, with the pair selling over a million of the software. Going to follow the remarkable success of VisiCalc, another group coached by Mitch Kapoor created Lotus 1-2-3, a new spreadsheet software, in 1983.

Mitch and his team filled Lotus 1-2-3 with graphing, rudimentary database capabilities, and charting along with simple programming. Lotus 1-2-3 became a new market favorite as a result of this.

While Microsoft had already released (in 1982) Multiplan, it was overshadowed by Lotus 1-2-3. This prompted Microsoft to create Excel, and the rest is history. Multiplan in 1982, Microsoft released Multiplan, a spreadsheet program that was very common on Control Application for small computers (CP/M systems) but lost ground to Lotus 1-2-3 on MS-DOS. This prompted the development of a modern spreadsheet known as Excel, which was created with the aim of doing everything 1-2-3 does, except faster and better. The first Mac edition of Excel was launched in 1985, followed by the 1st Windows version in Nov.1987.

Lotus took its time bringing 1-2-3 to Windows, so by 1988, Excel had begun to outsell 1-2-3, assisting Microsoft in becoming the dominant computer software maker. This achievement, which dethroned the emperor of the software world, established Microsoft as a legitimate rival and demonstrated its commitment to producing interactive software in the world. Microsoft maintained its lead by releasing new software every two years or so. Excel 11, commonly known as MS Office Excel 2021, is the most recent update for the Windows platform. Microsoft Excel 2023 is the most recent update for Mac OS X. (Office 2021 was released in early October 2021 for Windows and macOS)

Thanks to its ability to adjust to virtually any business method, MS Excel is the most familiar, scalable, and commonly adopted business software in the world today, with the new releases of Excel 2023 & Excel365. When used in conjunction with other MS Office software such as Outlook, PowerPoint & Word, there is little that this versatile mix cannot manage.

MS Excel and the Office Suite have almost infinite applications. Consider the following top ten list of Excel's most common and strong infrastructural development:

- Model and interpret almost all data efficiently
- Easily find the correct data points
- In one single cell, make a data chart.
- You can use the spreadsheets from wherever.
- As one works with others, they will connect, collaborate, and achieve more.
- Make use of Pivot Charts that are more interactive and dynamic.
- Make the data displays more sophisticated.
- Make it simpler and quicker.
- Increase the computing ability to create larger, more complicated spreadsheets.
- Use Excel Services to publish and distribute your work.

When one combines this with the ability to customize and optimize any operation using VBA, they have a powerful Business Intelligence platform, flexible and creative enough to address almost any business need.

1.6 BASIC EXCEL COMPONENTS

It's critical to know where everything is in the window when one starts using it. But, we'll go through all of the big components that one should be aware of before diving into the realm of Microsoft Excel.

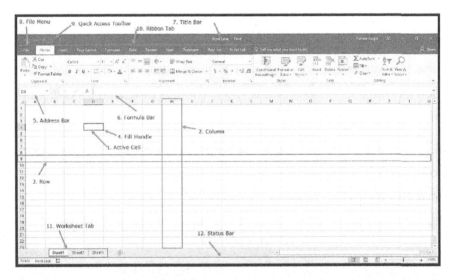

A cell that is selected is known as an active cell. A rectangular box will be used to illustrate it, and its name will be displayed in the address bar. Clicking on the cell or using the arrow keys can activate it. One can double-click on the cell or use the F2 key to edit it.

A column is the vertical grouping of cells. There are 16384 columns total on one single worksheet. From A till XFD, each column has its alphabet for identification. By clicking on a column's header, one can select it.

A row is the horizontal grouping of cells. One single worksheet may have up to 1048576 rows. For identification, each row has a unique number ranging from 1–1048576. By clicking on the row number on the left side of the browser, one can select it.

Fill Handle is the active cell's fill handle is a tiny dot in the right corner on the lower. It allows one to fill text sequences, ranges, serial numbers, and numeric values, among other things.

The Address Bar displays the active cell's address. If one picks more than one cell, the name of the 1st cell in the range will be shown.

Underneath the ribbon is the formula row, which is an input bar. It displays the contents of the active cell and allows one to type a formula into the cell. The workbook's name would appear in the title bar, accompanied by the program name (MS Excel).

The file menu, like many other programs, is a basic menu. It has choices such as (Save, Open, New, Save As, Excel Options, Print, Share, etc.).

1.6.1 ACCESS TOOLBAR (QUICK)

A toolbar that allows one to access the options easily they need the most. When introducing new choices to the easy access toolbar, one can select their favorite options.

1.6.2 RIBBON TAB

Beginning with Microsoft Excel 2007, all choice menus have been replaced by ribbons. Ribbon tabs are a set of various alternative groups that include additional options.

1.6.3 WORKSHEET COLUMN

This tab displays all of the worksheets in a workbook. Sheet1, 2, and 3 are the names of the 3 worksheets that will appear in the latest workbook by nature.

The Excel window's status bar is a small bar at the right. When one begins operating with Excel, it will have immediate assistance.

Edit the active cell	F2	^ U
Insert or edit comment	Shift F2	Fn ⇧ F2
Cancel entry	Esc	Esc
Select one character right	Shift →	⇧ →
Select one character left	Shift ←	⇧ ←
Move one word right	Ctrl →	^ →
Move one word left	Ctrl ←	^ ←
Select one word right	Ctrl Shift →	^ ⇧ →
Select one word left	Ctrl Shift ←	^ ⇧ ←
Select to beginning of cell	Shift Home	Fn ⇧ ←
Select to end of cell	Shift End	Fn ⇧ →
Delete to end of line	Ctrl Delete	^ Delete

BOOK 2
Understanding & Getting Started with Microsoft Excel

Since spreadsheets (Microsoft Excel) are so widely used, the chances are that someone, if you have ever worked on the computer, you have at least once used them. It had gone a long way from the invention of ABACUS in the 14th century.

Excel allows one to do pretty much anything.

- Using formulas and functions to perform logical operations.
- Use diagrams and charts to interpret the data further and uncover hidden patterns.
- Use Pivot tables to extract relevant details from a broad data set, filtering and sorting data to locate specific details.
- Use Macro to automate the reports. It is like a mini RPA bot.
- Use Visual Basic programming to make a custom program.
- Microsoft Excel is used for organizing, sorting, evaluating, and displaying results.
- One can insert data in Excel Cells as Strings, or Numerical Values, or Dates, and save the files for potential use.
- One can conduct calculations using a variety of Excel formulas
- You can build tools and dashboards and interact with other software.
- One can link to a variety of databases.
- One can visualize data in charts and can use pivot tables to dig down and analyze data.

Microsoft has published 29 new variants of Excel with three different operating systems over the past three decades, each one substantially different from the previous one.

2.1 WHAT IS THE BEST WAY TO USE MICROSOFT EXCEL?

In Excel, one does the job in a workbook. Each workbook has 1 or more spreadsheets/worksheets, each of which is made up of different cells that contain our results.

Before one makes the first Excel workbook, here's what they need to learn.

2.1.1 OPEN A NEW WORKBOOK

When one opens Excel on the computer, it immediately creates a fresh blank workbook.

To access a current workbook, select 'File' and then 'Open,' or use (control+N). It is a shortcut to open a new workbook.

To open an already opened workbook, select on file, then open, click on browser use browser to locate the needed workbook and click open.

2.1.2 INCLUDING A WORKSHEET

Every Excel workbook comes with three worksheets by design. By pressing the worksheet tabs right above the status bar, one will navigate the various worksheets.

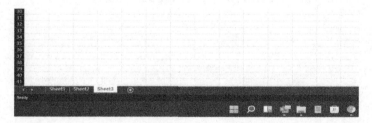

Tap the Insert Worksheet to the right of the current worksheet sections to add a fresh worksheet.

2.1.3 CHANGING THE NAME OF A WORKSHEET

To change a worksheet tab, use one of the following methods:

1st option: If one is using a computer, right-click the tab they want to change; if one is using a Mac, control-click the tab they want to rewrite. A menu with shortcuts would appear.

- From the shortcut menu, choose Rename.
- Fill in the current term name.
- Press.

2nd option: Hold the mouse over the page one intend to rename and double-click it.

To change the page, start typing.

Press.

2.1.4 USE THE RIBBON IN EXCEL

The ribbon in Excel gives commands. An order is an action taken by the operator. Creating a new document, printing the document, and so on are examples of commands. The ribbon in Excel 2023 can be seen in the picture below.

The ribbon is a top-mounted control pad. The Ribbon contains all of the materials one will need for their worksheet. To see what resources and buttons are accessible, click on each tab.

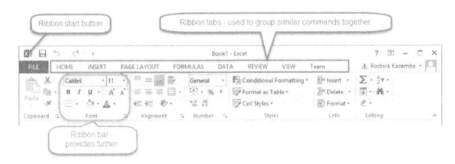

The start button of the ribbon is used to perform commands such as developing new documents, save the existing work, writing, print and using Excel's customization choices, among others.

2.1.5 RIBBON TABS

These tabs are also used to combine identical commands. Basic commands such as editing data to make it more presentable, to search and locating unique data inside the spreadsheet are performed on the home page.

2.1.6 RIBBON BAR

This bar is used to group identical commands. The Alignment ribbon bar, for example, is used to organize all of the instructions that are used to coordinate data together.

2.1.7 USING WORKSHEETS TO MANAGE DATA

In Excel, every workbook will have several worksheets, which are shown as tabs at the bottom of the page. By clicking the tab, one can open or delete a specific sheet. Using many worksheets is a simple way to store vast amounts of data in a logical fashion.

If one right-clicks on a tab, they see choices like rename and erase. A fresh blank worksheet is accessed when one presses the + button.

A spreadsheet is a set of columns and rows. A cell is formed when one row and one column intersect. Data is recorded in cells. A cell address is used to identify each cell individually. Letters are used to mark columns, and numbers are used to label arcs.

A workbook is a list of worksheets. A workbook in Excel has three cells by nature. To fit the requirements, one can erase or add more sheets. One should rename the sheets to something more important, like Daily Expenses or Annual Budget, for example.

It's time to enter some details.

One can add data into a cell when they pick it and start typing. Letters, equations, and Numbers are only a few examples of data types. One may also copy and paste data from other sites.

2.1.8 DOING CALCULATIONS

One may use operators like +, -, *, /, and others to perform several functions on sets, numbers, and other items, such as addition, multiplication, division, and subtraction.

2.1.9 CARRYING OUT MEASUREMENTS

A function is a formula that has already been specified; one may enter the formula in the empty cell. Begin the formula with an equal sign (=). Then, in parentheses, type the function and the cell names on which one wants to execute these functions. The formula will be shown in the ribbon's formula bar. For e.g., if one wants to find the number of data in two separate cells, such as A2 & B2, they can use the formula =SUM (A2:B2).

Make a copy of your workbook and share it with others.

When one is done with the spreadsheet, click Ctrl+S to save it.

To transfer the excel workbook through OneDrive, either send it to the cloud, press the share button in the top right corner of the window.

2.2 CUSTOMIZATION MICROSOFT EXCEL ENVIRONMENT

Many people prefer a black color setting.

If blue is the favorite color, one can make the theme color appear blue as well. One will not want to use ribbon tabs such as developer if they are not a programmer. Any of this is possible thanks to customizations. One can make these changes:

- Customizing the ribbon.
- Choosing a color scheme.
- Formula settings.
- Settings for proofing.
- Save the settings.

2.3 CUSTOMIZATION OF THE RIBBON

Let's begin with the ribbon customization. Let's say one does not want to see any of the tabs on the toolbar, or they want to include some additional tabs, like the developer tab. They will do this by using the options window.

- Choose the ribbon's start button.

- From the dropdown menu, choose options. One must be able to see a dialogue box called Excel Options.

- From the left-hand side screen, pick the customize ribbon option, as seen below. • Delete the checkpoints from the tabs on the right-hand side that one does not want to see on the ribbon. Review, display tabs, and Page Layout have been omitted from this example.

When you're done, click the "OK" icon.

This is how the ribbon would appear.

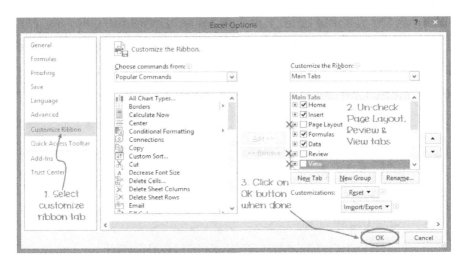

2.3.1 CUSTOMIZING THE RIBBON'S TABS

One may also create their tab, call it whatever they want, and allocate it commands. Let's make a tab with the text (anything you want) in the ribbon.

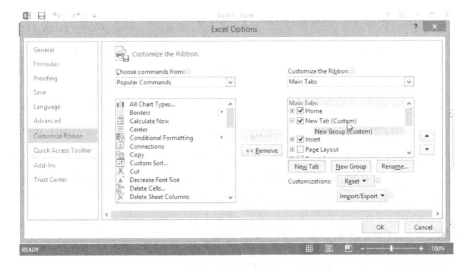

- Pick Customize the Ribbon from the context menu by right-clicking on the ribbon. A discussion window similar to the one seen above will emerge.

- As seen in the animated picture below, click the new tab icon.

38

- Go to the newly formed tab and choose it.

- Choose the Rename option.

- Assign it the name ——————

- Under the ————— tab, choose New Group (Custom), as seen in the image below.

- Click the Rename icon and assign it to My Commands.

- Let's move on to adding commands to the ribbon bar.

- On the center panel, one will see a list of commands.

- Press the 'Add' button after selecting the 'All chart styles' command.

- Choose OK.

This is how the ribbon would appear.

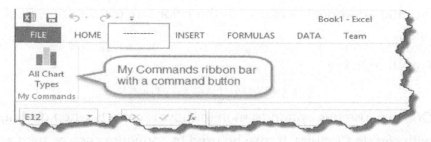

2.3.2 CHOOSING A COLOR SCHEME

To change the color theme of an Excel board, go to the Excel ribbon and select the File Options button. It will open the window where one must complete the steps below.

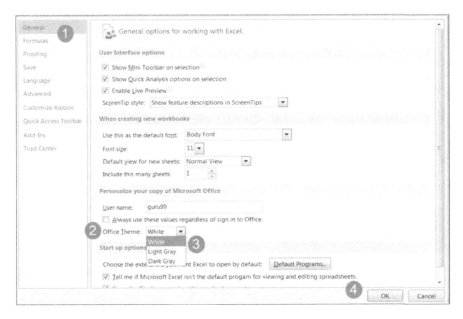

The left-hand panel's basic tab would be picked by default.

Go to Excel's General Choices and look for the color scheme.

Pick the appropriate color from the color scheme dropdown column.

Press the OK key.

2.3.3 FORMULAS' SETTINGS

One may use this option to monitor how Excel acts when dealing with certain formulas. It may be used to configure choices such as autocomplete while entering formulas, changing the cell referencing type, and using numbers for rows and columns, among other things.

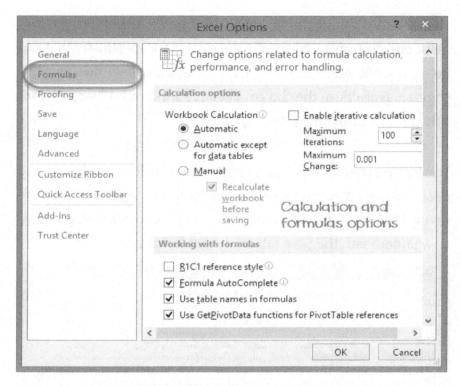

To make a choice, tick the box next to it. Remove the checkmark from the checkbox to disable a choice. This alternative is available in the Options dialogue box, under the Formulas tab on the column (on the left side).

2.4 PROOFING SETTINGS

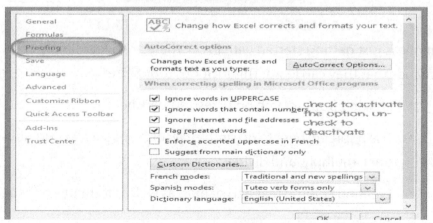

This choice changes the text that has been inserted into Excel. It helps one customize things like the dictionary vocabulary that can be used while searching for misspellings, dictionary tips, etc. This choice is available in the choices dialogue window on the left-hand-side column, under the proofing tab.

2.4.1 SAVE YOUR PREFERENCES

This feature enables one to set the standard file format while saving data and permit auto-recovery if the computer shuts down before saving the job. This choice is available in the Choices dialogue window underneath the Save tab on the left-hand-side screen.

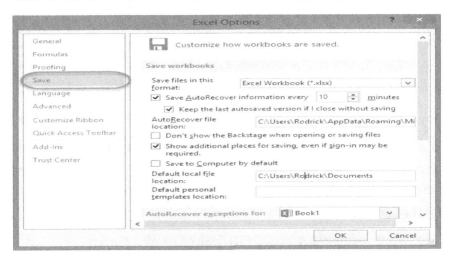

2.5 BASICS OF THE MICROSOFT EXCEL

If one is just getting started with Excel, there are a few simple commands that they can learn. This includes topics like:

- Starting from scratch on a fresh spreadsheet.

- Use a spreadsheet to do simple calculations such as add, subtract, multiply, and divide.

- Creating column text and names, as well as formatting them.

- Excel's auto-fill capabilities.

- Add tables, rows, and spreadsheets may be or deleted. We'll go into how to incorporate stuff like several columns and rows in the sections below.

- In a spreadsheet, keep column and row names clear as one click past them, so they know what data is filled as they go away from the page.

2.5.1 INSERTING ROWS OR COLUMNS

When one is working on their results, they will notice that they need to add further rows and columns on a regular basis. It's possible that one will need to insert hundreds of rows at times. It would be very repetitive to do this one by one. Luckily, there will always be an easier option.

To add several rows or columns to a spreadsheet, choose the exact no. of already existing columns or rows as the number of rows or columns one wishes to add. Then select "Insert" from the right-click menu.

We have added three more rows—spreadsheet by selecting three rows and then pressing insert.

2.5.2 USING PIVOT TABLES FOR DATA

In a database, pivot tables are being used to reorganize information. They won't adjust the data, but they can add up values or compare various pieces of data in the spreadsheet if that's what one would like.

Here is an example. For instance, if one wants to see how many students are in each class house. One may think that this example has not much data, but this will be beneficial with larger data sets.

Go to Data, then to Pivot Table to make the Pivot Table. Excel can populate the Pivot Table for you immediately, but one can still rearrange the files. And you have a choice of four choices.

2.5.2.1 REPORT FILTER

One can use this to look at just specific rows in the dataset. For e.g., instead of including all students in the filter, you might choose to include students in a certain house.

2.5.2.2 COLUMN LABELS

This may be the dataset's headers.

2.5.2.3 ROW LABELS

This may be the dataset's rows. Data from the columns can be seen in both row & column names (such as the First Name can be pulled to the Row or Column label, it depends on how one wants to see the data.)

2.5.2.4 VALUE

This segment encourages one to take a different approach to the data. One can total, count, avg, min, count amounts, and perform a few other operations on the data instead of just bringing in some statistical value. In reality, by definition, one drags a field to Value; it often does a count.

You will go to the Pivot Table and move the House column to the Row Labels and Values since we wanted to count the number of students in every house. This will add up to the no. of students affiliated with each house.

2.5.3 AUTOFILL

There are many ways to use this function, but a fill handle is more straightforward. Choose the cells one wants to be the source, then look for a fill handle in the corner (lower-right) of a cell and move it to cover the cells one may want to fill, or simply double-click.

	C	D	E	F	G	
	Description	Views	Leads	View to Lead	Links	H1 C
	Vivamus porta elit place	430	0	0.00%	0	
	Morbi tincidunt metus u	372	0	0.00%	4	
	Mauris ut accumsan erc	302	1	0.33%	1	
	Fusce fermentum tincid	294	0	0.00%	1	
	Nullam luctus nibh puru	378	2	0.53%	0	
	Pellentesque habitant n	469	0	0.00%	4	
	Morbi vestibulum dolor	226	4	1.77%	0	
	Morbi id quam lacus.	201	0	0.00%	7	
	Aliquam ornare, eros ac	333	0	0.00%	3	
	Vivamus quis nulla dui.	104	5	4.81%	0	
	Nullam pharetra sem eu	530	0	0.00%	1	
	Lorem ipsum dolor sit a	150	10	6.67%	1	

fx =E2/D2

2.5.4 FILTERS

When working with large amounts of data (as businesses frequently do), one does not always need to look at each row at the same time. One may occasionally only want to examine the data that meets specific criteria. Filters help in this manner.

Filters help one to narrow down the data so that they only see specific rows at a time. Each column in the data can have a filter applied to it in Excel. One can then decide which cells they want to see all at once.

For example, by going to the Data tab and choosing "Filter," one can pick whether they want the data to be ordered in descending or ascending order, as well as which rows they want to see.

For example, if one selects a specific house for students, the other houses will disappear. The other rows vanish as you click the filter.

When a filter is on, copy/paste the values in the spreadsheet to perform further research in another spreadsheet.

2.5.5 SORT

One may come across a collection of data that hasn't been organized in any way. Perhaps one exported a list of business contacts or a set of blog entries. In any event, Excel's sort function can assist in alphabetizing any list.

To arrange the data in a column, click on it. Then, in the toolbar's "Data" column, look for a "Sort" choice on the left. If A is first, then "Z," one has to press on it once. Click the icon twice if "Z" is positioned above "A." When the "A" is positioned above the "Z," the chart will be ordered alphabetically. If the "Z" is positioned above the "A," the chart would be ordered in the opposite alphabetical order.

2.5.6 REMOVE DUPLICATES

Duplicate material is more common in larger datasets. One may have a set of different connections in an organization and just want to know how many they have. Getting rid of duplicates is essential in cases like these.

To get rid of duplicates, choose the row or column one wish to get rid of them from. Then click "Remove Duplicates" from the Data tab (underneath Tools). A pop-up would appear asking you to check which details you intend to use. Simply choose "Remove Duplicates" and done.

This function can also be used to erase an entire row depending on the duplicate values of the column. As if one has three rows of details about a movie and just needs to see 1, they can pick all datasets and then delete duplicates. The final list can only include specific titles, with no duplicates.

2.5.7 PASTE SPECIAL

Frequently, one will want to convert the elements in a data row or into a column. Copying and pasting each individual header will take a long time. Not to mention that one might potentially fall victim to one of the most common and costly Excel pitfalls: human failure.

Enable Excel to do the heavy lifting for you. Go ahead and choose the column or row that one wants to transfer. Copy by right-clicking and selecting "Copy." Then, in the spreadsheet, pick the cells where one wants the first row or column to start. Select "Paste Special" from the context menu after right-clicking on the cell. Select the choice to translate when the module appears.

Paste Special is one of those functions that people use over and over again. One may also opt to copy formulas, formats, even column widths or values in the module. This is particularly useful when copying the results of the pivot table into a structured and graphed chart.

2.5.8 TEXT TO COLUMNS

What if one wants to divide data from a single cell into 2 separate cells? For instance, one may want to extract someone's company name from the email address. One may want to split anyone's full name into their first and last name for the email marketing models.

All scenarios are possible due to Excel. To begin, select the column one wants to divide. Then, on the Data page, use "Text to Columns." A tab with more details would appear. To begin, choose between "Delimited" and "Fixed Width."

- "Delimited" indicates one wants the column to be broken up by characters like commas, tabs, or spaces.
- "Fixed Width" indicates one gets to choose the same place in all of the columns where the break will happen.

For example, use "Delimited" in the example below to divide the complete name into first & last names.

The delimiters must therefore be chosen. A tab, comma, void, or semicolon character could be included here. ("anything else" might, for instance, be the "@" sign in the email address.) Afterward, Excel will show the preview of how one new column will appear.

When one is done with the preview, click "Next." This page would encourage one to choose Advanced Formats if they want to. Select "Finish" when they are done.

2.5.9 FORMAT PAINTER

As one has already noticed, Excel has a range of characteristics that render analyzing numbers and analyzing data fast and straightforward. However, if one has ever spent time customizing a sheet, they know how boring it can be.

Don't spend time repeatedly entering the same formatting instructions. To quickly copy the format from 1 section of the worksheet to another, just use the format painter. To use it, select a cell one wants to duplicate, then go to the top toolbar and select the format painter choice.

BOOK 3
Formulas & Functions of the Microsoft Excel

Excel formulas enable one to find associations among values in the spreadsheet's cells, conduct mathematical calculations with those values, and then display the outcome in the cell of their choosing. Sum, ratio, aggregation, subtraction, average, and times, dates are among the formulas that can be performed automatically.

3.1 USES IN FINANCE AND ACCOUNTING

Excel is widely employed in the banking and accounting fields. In reality, many businesses depend solely on Excel worksheets for their budgeting, planning, and accounting needs.

Although Excel is an "information" processing software, the most popular data that is handled is financial data. Excel is the best financial app, according to people who do financial analysis. Although several parts of financial software are designed to execute complex functions, Excel's solidity and accessibility are its best features. Excel templates should be as efficient as the analyst wants.

Excel is used by accountants, managers, consultants, investors, and individuals in all aspects of financial careers to fulfill their everyday tasks.

3.2 BASIC TERMS IN EXCEL

In Excel, there are 2 primary methods for doing calculations: functions & formulas.

3.2.1 FORMULAS

A formula in MS Excel is an equation that works on values in a number of cells or a single cell. For e.g., =B1+B2+B3 calculates the number of values in cells B1 through B3.

3.2.2 FUNCTIONS

In Excel, functions are predetermined formulas. They do take away the time-consuming manual entry of formulas by assigning them Easy titles. =SUM, for instance (B1:B3). The feature adds up all of the values in the range B1 to B3.

The Feature Collection on the Formulas tab contains all usable Excel functions:

3.3 HOW TO USE FUNCTIONS & FORMULAS

Excel has over 400 functions, and the amount is increasing from time to time. Of course, memorizing any of them is almost difficult, and one does not have to. The Function tab can assist you in finding the function that is the ideal fit for a given role. In contrast, Excel Formula Intelligence will guide you with the function's syntax and reasons as soon as one enters the function's name in the cell, followed by an equal sign:

	A	B	C
1	1	2	4
2			
3	=sum(		
4	SUM(**number1**, [number2], ...)		

Write a Formula.

Follow the instructions below to insert a formula.

- Choose a cell to work with.

- Type the equal sign (=) to tell Excel what formula to enter in the cell.

- Write the formula A1+A2 as an illustration.

A3	▼	⋮	×	✓	f_x	=A1+A2		
	A	B	C	D	E	F	
1	2						
2	3						
3	5						
4							

To save time, choose cells A1 & A2 instead of writing A1 & A2.

- Increase cell A1's value to three.

	A	B	C	D	E	F
A1				f_x	3	

	A	B	C	D	E	F
1	3					
2	3					
3	6					
4						

Excel immediately recalculates the data of cell A3. One of the most important features of MS Excel is this.

3.3.1 MAKE CHANGES TO THE FORMULA

Excel displays the value or the formula of the cell in the formula bar as one selects it.

	A	B	C	D	E	F
A3				f_x	=A1+A2	

	A	B	C	D	E	F
1	2					
2	3					
3	5					
4						

One can change the formula by changing it in the bar and press enter.

	A	B	C	D	E	F
SUMIF				f_x	=A1-A2	

	A	B	C	D	E	F
1	2					
2	3					
3	=A1-A2					
4						

3.4 BASIC EXCEL FORMULAS

These are some basic formulas in excel, and one should know to make working in Excel easier.

3.5 SUM

The function of SUM is the 1st Excel formula that one can learn. =SUM is an essential simple formula to know since it helps one add quantities in various ways. Excel quickly performs this formula, but some tricks to =SUM still offer more data-adding capabilities.

To begin, =SUM will sum whole rows of no. or only specific cells inside a row. Here's an example of what it feels like:

Values from chosen columns or rows set are normally aggregated.

Formula.

=SUM (no. 1, [no. 2],...)

=SUM (B2:G2), for example, is a basic collection that sums the quantities of the row.

A basic selection that sum the values of the column is =SUM (A2:A8)

=SUM (A3:A7, A10, A13:A17) It is a collection that sum values from a range of A3 to A7, does not add A8, adds A10, does not add A11 & A12, and adds ranges from A13 to A17.

=SUM (A3:A9)/21—this collection shows that one can turn the function in a formula

	A	B	C
1	**Country**	**Population**	
2	China	1,389,618,778	
3	India	1,311,559,204	
4	USA	331,883,986	
5	Indonesia	264,935,824	
6	Pakistan	210,797,836	
7	Brazil	210,301,591	
8	Nigeria	208,679,114	
9	Bangladesh	161,062,905	
10	Russia	141,944,641	
11	Mexico	127,318,112	
12	**Total**	=SUM(B2:B11)	Output = 4,358,101,991
13			
14			

3.6 SUBTRACTION

In Excel, insert those cells one is subtracting in the format =SUM to execute the subtraction formula (B1, -C1). By inserting the negative sign before that cell, one is subtracting, and they may use the SUM formula to deduct it. For e.g., if B1 is 12 and C1 is -5, =SUM (B1, -C1) performs 12 + -5 and the outcome is 7.

Subtracting, including percentages, lacks its function or formula in Excel, but it doesn't suggest it can't be achieved. There are two ways to deduct specific values (or values inside the cells).

Formula

Used the same formula =SUM. Enter the cells one wants to deduct in the format =SUM (B1, -C1), with a minus sign (written with a hyphen) before a cell whose meaning one wants to subtract. To get the result, between the two cells in parentheses, press enter.

Write =B1-C1 in the format. To deduct several values from each other, type an equal's symbol, then the first value of the cell, a minus sign, and the value one wants to subtract. Press enter.

C2			f_x	=SUM(B2, -A2)		
	A		B		C	D
1	Value 1		Value 2		Result	
2		75		85		10
3						
4						
5						

3.7 DIVISION

To use the division formula in Excel, type =B1/C1 into the cells one wants to divide. To differentiate cell B1 by 1C, this formula uses a forward cut, "/." For e.g., if B1 is 5 and C1 is 10, the decimal value returned by =A1/B1 is 0.5.

SUM			f_x	=B2/A2	
	A		B		C
1	Value 1		Value 2		Result
2		75		85	=B2/A2
3					
4					

One of the most basic operations one will do in Excel is division. To do so, select an empty cell, type an equals symbol, "=," and then the two values (or more) one wants to divide, separated by a forward dash, "/." As seen in the snapshot below, the outcome should be in the format =B2/A2.

When one press Enter, the ideal quotient will display in the highlighted cell.

3.8 MULTIPLICATION

In Excel, insert the cells ONE IS multiplying in the template =B1*C1 to execute the multiplication. An asterisk is used in this calculation to multiply cell B1 by cell C1. For e.g., if B1 is 10 and C1 is 5, the result of =B1*C1 is 50.

One might believe that multiplying variables in Excel will have its own formula or that the "x" character is used to indicate the multiplication of multiple values. That's as easy as using an asterisk *.

	A	B	C	D	E
	SUM ▲▼ ✗ ✓ ƒx =A2*B2*C2				
	A	B	C	D	E
1	Value 1	Value 2	Value 3	Result	
2	75	85	95	=A2*B2*C2	
3					
4					
5					

Highlight a blank cell in an Excel file to multiply 2 or more values. Next, in the format, =B1*1*C1..., set the data or cells one wants to multiply together. Each number in the formula would be effectively multiplied by the asterisk.

To return the desired order, press Enter. Take a peek at the screenshot above to see how this works.

3.9 PERCENTAGE

To use the % formula in Excel, type =B1/C1 into the cells one wants to find a percentage for. Highlight a cell, go to the Home tab, and pick "Percentage" from the dropdown menu to translate the decimal value to a %.

While there isn't a specific Excel "formula" for %, Excel makes it simple to transform the amount of a cell into a percentage, so one is not stuck estimating and attempting to enter the numbers.

The Home tab of excel contains the fundamental setting for converting a cell's worth to a percentage. Select the tab, highlight the cell or cells one wants to convert to a %, and choose Conditional Formatting from the dropdown menu next to it (the menu button could say "General" before). Then, from the dropdown menu that emerges, choose "Percentage." The meaning of each cell one has highlighted will be converted to a percentage. This element can be found farther down.

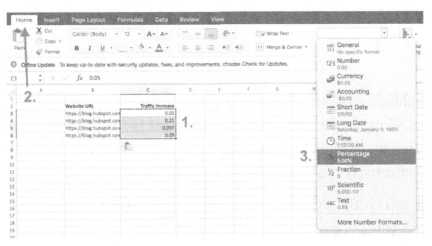

Please remember that if one uses other formulas just like the division formula (such as =A1/B1) to make new values, the results appear as decimals by design. Merely select the cells and change their type to "Percentage" from the tab before or after performing this algorithm, as seen above.

3.10 RANDOM NUMBERS GENERATOR

Using =RANDBETWEEN in the worksheet, one can conveniently pick random numbers (SELECT VALUES).

	A	B	C
1	Name	Random Number	
2	Sarah Anderson	4	
3	Adam Michaels		
4	Dante France		
5	Jordan Song	CONGRATULATIONS	
6	Jip Kirkland	DANTE!	
7	Kerry Proffit		
8	Lawrence Walker		
9	Maria Ramos		
10			

As seen in the illustration, one may use this formula to select numbers from the data in the worksheet.

Another use of this algorithm is to choose the winner from the list of 100 names by instructing Excel to select from the winning lines.

3.11 TIPS FOR USING FUNCTION CORRECTLY

3.11.1 INSERTION OF FUNCTION

The configuration of each function is the same. SUM, for instance (A1:A4). SUM is the title of this function. The section between the parentheses (arguments) indicates that we are giving Excel the range A1:A4. The labels in the cells A1, A2, A3, & A4 are added using this function. It is difficult to recall which function to use for what job and which arguments to use. Luckily, Excel's Insert Function functionality will assist you.

Conduct the steps below to insert the function.

- Choose a cell to work with.

- Select Insert Function from the dropdown menu.

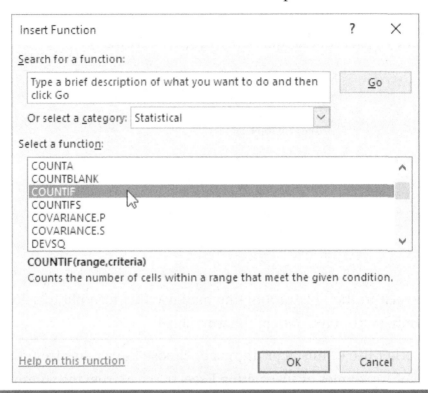

The dialogue box for 'Insert Function' emerges.

- Look for a function or choose one from the category. Select COUNTIF from the Statistical classification, for instance.
- Choose OK.
- The dialogue box for 'Function Arguments' opens.
- Pick the A1:C2 set in the Range box by clicking on it.
- Type >5 in the Criteria window, then click OK.

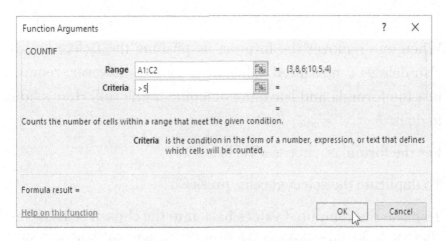

As a result, COUNTIF calculates the number of cells in a row that are higher than 5.

	A	B	C	D	E	F
1	3	8	6	3		
2	10	5	4			
3						

D1 → : × ✓ *fx* =COUNTIF(A1:C2,">5")

Start typing =COUNTIF (A1:C2, ">5") rather than using the Insert Function option. Rather than typing A1:C2, pick the range A1:C2 when one gets to =COUNTIF (.

Rather than retyping the same solution in different cells, copy it.

There's no reason to keep typing a formula into the cell if you've already typed it in once. Start dragging the fill handle to nearby cells to transfer the formula (a little square at the right-hand (lower) corner of a cell). Place the cursor over the fill handle, double-click the plus sign to transfer the formula to the entire column.

3.11.2 REMOVE THE FORMULA BUT KEEP THE RESULT

When one removes the formula by pushing the Delete key, it also deletes a measured value. You should, however, remove just the formula and leave the outcome in the cell. Here's how to do it:

For the formulas, choose all cells.

To duplicate the selected cells, press Ctrl + C.

To paste the computed values back into the chosen cells, right-click the selection and choose Paste Values from Values. Alternatively, click Shift+F10, then V to use the Paste Special short-cut.

3.11.3 OPERATOR PRECEDENCE

The order for which calculations are performed in Excel is set by default. If a portion of the formula is enclosed in brackets, it will be computed first. After that, it calculates multiplication and division. When this is done, Excel will add, then subtract the rest of the formula. Have a look at the illustration below.

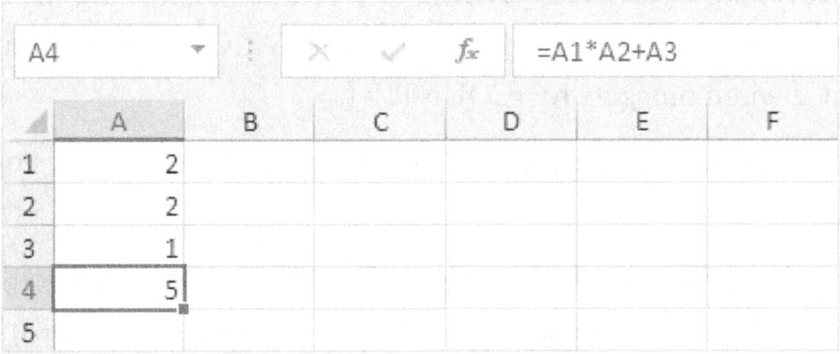

A4		✕ ✓ f_x	=A1*A2+A3		
	A	B	C	D	E	F
1	2					
2	2					
3	1					
4	5					
5						

Excel starts by multiplying the numbers (A1 * A2). The data of cell A3 is then added to this result by Excel.

As an alternative,

A4		⋮	✕	✓	*fx*	=A1*(A2+A3)	

◢	A	B	C	D	E	F
1	2					
2	2					
3	1					
4	6					
5						

Excel first calculates the portion in brackets (A2+A3). The product is then multiplied by the amount of cell A1.

3.11.4 DO NOT USE DUAL QUOTES TO ENCLOSE AMOUNTS

"Quotation marks" ought to be used to accompany every text in the Excel formulas. If one doesn't want Excel to handle numbers as text values, then do not do the quotation marks.

For, e.g., one might place the following formula in cell C2 to verify the value in cell B2 and returning 1 if it is "Passed," and 0 otherwise:

=IF (B2="pass", 1, 0)

If one copies the formula to other cells, they will have a column of 1s, 0s that can be measured without difficulty.

Consider what happens if the numbers are double-quoted:

=IF (B2="pass", "1", "0")

The output appears to be normal at first glance, with the very same column of 1s & 0s. Even so, a closer examination reveals that the resultant values are by far left-aligned in the cells, indicating that they are numeric strings rather than numbers. If anyone tries to quantify the 1s and 0s afterward, they may wind up tearing their skin out, trying to find out why a perfectly right Sum or Count formula returns empty.

C2 ▾ ⋮	=IF(B2="pass", 1, 0) ✓	C2 ▾ ⋮ =IF(B2="pass", "1", "0") ✗

	A	B	C	D
1	Name		Result	
2	Ava	Fail	0	
3	Aiden	Pass	1	
4	Jackson	Fail	0	
5	Liam	Pass	1	
6	Sophia	Pass	1	
7	Lucas	Pass	1	
8	Passed		4 =SUM(C2:C7)	

	A	B	C	D
1	Name		Result	
2	Ava	Fail	0	
3	Aiden	Pass	1	
4	Jackson	Fail	0	
5	Liam	Pass	1	
6	Sophia	Pass	1	
7	Lucas	Pass	1	
8	Passed		0 =SUM(C2:C7)	

3.11.5 COPY/PASTE THE FORMULA

Excel changes the cell references for every new cell the formula is copied to as one copies a formula. Follow the measures below to get a better understanding of this.

1. Fill in cell A4 with the formula.

A4	▾	⋮	✕	✓	*fx*	=A1*(A2+A3)	

	A	B	C	D	E	F
1	2	5				
2	2	6				
3	1	4				
4	6					
5						

. Right-click cell A4, then do Copy (or do CTRL + c)...

...then, right-click cell B4 and pick Paste from the Options for paste menu (or hold CTRL + v).

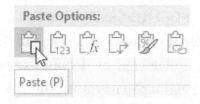

2b. The formula can also be dragged to cell B4. Select cell A4, then move it over to cell B4 by clicking on the right corner on the lower side of cell A4. This is far less time-consuming and produces the same results.

A4			×	✓	*fx*	=A1*(A2+A3)

	A	B	C	D	E	F
1	2	5				
2	2	6				
3	1	4				
4	6					
5						

As a consequence, the values in column B are referenced by the formula in cell B4.

B4			×	✓	*fx*	=B1*(B2+B3)

	A	B	C	D	E	F
1	2	5				
2	2	6				
3	1	4				
4	6	50				
5						

3.11.6 IN EXCEL FORMULAS, DO NOT FORMAT NUMBERS

Please note to enter no into the Excel calculations without any coding, such as a dollar sign or decimal separator. The comma is the standard claim separator in America and several other nations, and the dollar sign ($) is used to render utter cell references. It's possible that using certain characters in numbers would make Excel insane. Especially, rather than typing $2,000, type 2000, and then use a customized Excel number file to format the performance value to your preference.

In the calculations, make sure that both of the opening and closing brackets are the same.

One will need more than one collection of brackets to describe the order of calculations when creating a critical Excel formula for one or more clustered functions. Make sure that the brackets are correctly paired in those calculations, and closing brackets should have opening parenthesis. When one joins or modifies a formula, Excel shades bracket pairs of the same colors to make the task simpler.

3.11.7 CHECK THAT CALCULATION OPTIONS IS SET TO AUTO-MATIC

If one's Excel formulas have suddenly stopped recalculating themselves, the Calculation Options have most likely been changed to Manual. To correct this, select the Formulas tab, then to the Calculation group, pick Automatic from the Calculation Options button.

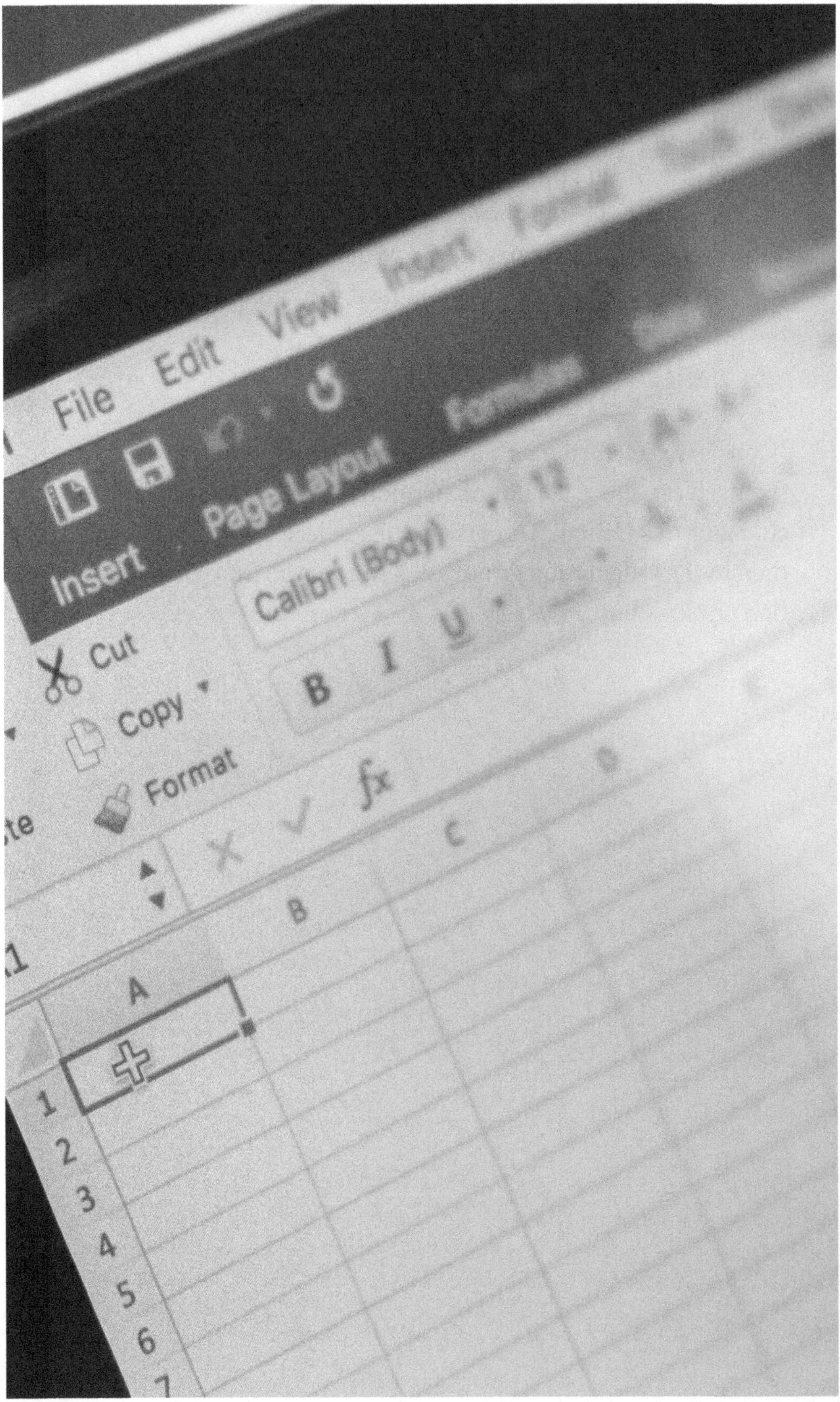
File
Edit
View
Insert
Insert
Page Layout
Cut
Copy
Format
Calibri (Body)
B
I
U
fx
A
B
C
1
2
3
4
5
6

BOOK 4
MS Excel Text's Functions

0,000.00	$125,000.00	$275,000.00
2,000.00	$190,000.00	$140,000.0
000.00	$435,000.00	$650,000.0
00.00)	($135,000.00)	$350,000.
0%	0%	10

[Segment Name]	[Segment Na

4.1 CONCATENATE

=CONCATENATE is a valuable formula for combining values from different cells into a single cell. As one needs to merge data from different cells into another cell, this formula saves one time & frustration. Instead of having to do it by hand, =CONCATENATE will do it in less time and with half the number of clicks.

Column A contains initial names, and Column B contains final names in this case. Those cells can be conveniently merged by writing

Formula.

=CONCATENATE (SELECT CELL, SELECT CELL), as seen in Column D, where the complete names are in the exact cell that one wanted. Consider how much copying and pasting this valuable formula has just saved you.

	A	B	C	D
1	First	Last	Formula	Answer
2	Sarah	Anderson	=CONCATENATE(A2,B2)	Sarah Anderson
3	Adam	Michaels		Adam Michaels
4	Dante	France		Dante France
5	Jordan	Song		Jordan Song
6	Jip	Kirkland		Jip Kirkland
7	Kerry	Proffit		Kerry Proffit
8	Lawrence	Walker		Lawrence Walker
9	Maria	Ramos		Maria Ramos

4.2 LEFT, MID, & RIGHT

Let's presume one has a line of text inside the cell that they want to split down into few separate parts. Instead of physically copy-pasting every piece of the script into its specific column, users could use a set of sequence functions to dismantle the sequence as required: LEFT, MID, and RIGHT.

4.2.1 LEFT

Reason: Used to retrieve the first (any) characters or numbers in the cell.

The formula is as follows: =LEFT (text, number of characters)

Text is the sequence that one wants to remove from.

The number of characters: it is the number of characters that one wants to remove beginning from the left-most word.

In the case below, one entered =LEFT(A2,4) in cell B2 and copy it into B3:B6. That helped them to retrieve the first four characters of the text.

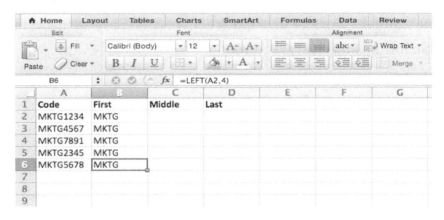

4.2.2 MID

Reason: it is used to separate characters or no's in the center depending on location.

The formula is as follow =MID (text, start position, number of characters)

Text is the sequence that one wants to remove from.

Start position: This is where one wants to start extraction from the sequence. The first place in the string, for instance, is 1.

The no. of characters one wants to remove is defined by a number of characters.

Such as typed =MID(A2,6,7) in cell B2 and copy it to B3:B6 in this case. We were able to remove the 2 numbers beginning in the 6th location of the code as a result of this.

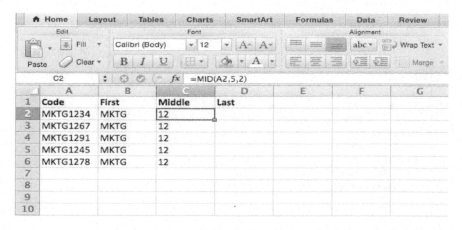

4.2.3 RIGHT

The last (any) no. of characters in a cell are extracted using this function.

The formula is as follows: =RIGHT (text, number of characters)

Text is the sequence from which one wants to extract information.

The number of characters: Beginning from the right-most character, the number of characters one intends to extract.

For this case, typed =RIGHT(A2,2) in cell B2 and copied it to cells B3:B6. We were able to retrieve the script's final two numbers as a result of this.

Edit | Font | Alignment

Fill | Calibri (Body) | 12 | A⁺ A⁻ | abc⁻ | Wrap Text ⁻

Paste | Clear ⁻ | B I U | | A ⁻ | | Merge ⁻

D6 | fx | =RIGHT(A6,2)

	A	B	C	D	E	F	G
1	Code	First	Middle	Last			
2	MKTG1234	MKTG	12	34			
3	MKTG1267	MKTG	12	67			
4	MKTG1291	MKTG	12	91			
5	MKTG1245	MKTG	12	45			
6	MKTG1278	MKTG	12	78			
7							
8							
9							
10							

4.3 TRIM

This TRIM function ensures that disruptive spaces do not cause errors in the functions. It means that there are no vacant spaces. TRIM only works on a single cell, unlike many functions that may work on a group of cells. As a result, it has the drawback of duplicating details in the spreadsheet.

If one copies and pastes data into a worksheet, it's possible that the pasted data would be jumbled. That means it may include extra spaces or secret characters, which would trigger calculations to fail because Excel requires data to be clean and free of disruptive spaces.

=TRIM clears out the pasted data so it can be included in Excel.

The animals in the cells in the illustration below have spaces at the start. It can be fixed by using the formula:

=TRIM (HIGHLIGHT A CELL).

	A	B	C
1	Data 1	Formula	Answer
2	Alpaca	=TRIM(A2)	Alpaca
3	Buffalo		Buffalo
4	Banteng		Banteng
5	Cow		Cow
6	Cat		Cat
7	Chicken		Chicken
8	Camel		Camel
9	Donkey		Donkey
10	Dog		Dog
11	Duck		Duck
12	Emu		Emu

4.4 LEN

This function is used if one wants to know how many characters are in the cell:

Formula

=LEN (your text)

If one wants to see how many characters, there are in cell A2? Simply write the formula in the new cell:

=LEN (B2)

It's important to remember that the Excel LEN feature counts all characters, even spaces:

C2	▼	:	=LEN(A2)

	A	B	C
1	Data		Len formula
2	1 apple		7
3	2 apples		8
4	35 apples		9

4.5 PROPER

Excel can be used for more than just data analysis; it can also be used to organize and filter data. =PROPER is a perfect formula to carry in the mind when typing vast volumes of data into Excel since it transforms the cell of the text to a proper case, in which the 1st letter of every phrase is capitalized. In contrast, the majority of the letters are not capitalized.

Many of the names in A (column) are not capitalized in the illustration. As one can see in D (Column), instead of clicking in every cell, removing the 1st letter of every word, and typing in a capitalized manner (it will take a long time and effort), =PROPER does it immediately.

	A	B	C	D
1	Data		Formula	Answer
2	Anna		=Proper(A2)	Anna
3	lauren			Lauren
4	Donte			Donte
5	john			John
6	patricia			Patricia
7	miquel			Miquel
8	Eleanor			Eleanor

To use this formula, do =Proper (selected cell)

4.6 SEARCH FUNCTION

If one wants to locate a text string inside another text string, the Excel SEARCH function is used. This function can be used to search, as the name suggests, locates a text string inside another text string with little consideration, for instance.

In your query, use wildcards.

Inside the search document, specify a start number.

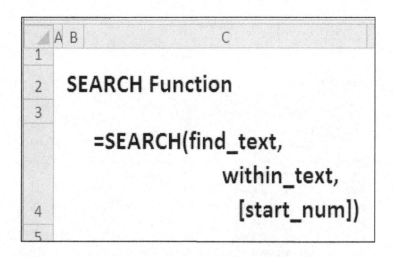

SEARCH (find_ text, within_ text, start_ no.)

- The text one is searching for in the found text.
- The string one is looking in is within the text.
- If the start number is not specified, the quest will begin with the 1st character.
- SEARCH reports the location of the match in a cell being scanned as it detects one.
- When the quest fails to locate a match, the #VALUE error is returned.
- SEARCH will return several results since we've given it multiple things to search for.

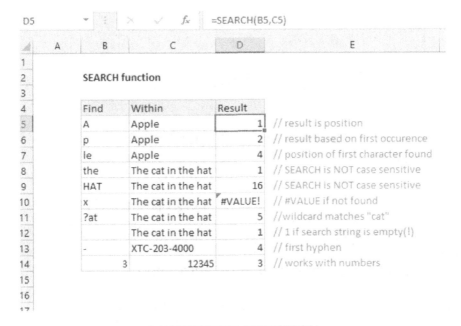

| | D5 | ▾ | : | × | ✓ | *fx* | =SEARCH(B5,C5) | |

▲	A	B	C	D	E
1					
2		SEARCH function			
3					
4		Find	Within	Result	
5		A	Apple	1	// result is position
6		p	Apple	2	// result based on first occurence
7		le	Apple	4	// position of first character found
8		the	The cat in the hat	1	// SEARCH is NOT case sensitive
9		HAT	The cat in the hat	16	// SEARCH is NOT case sensitive
10		x	The cat in the hat	#VALUE!	// #VALUE if not found
11		?at	The cat in the hat	5	//wildcard matches "cat"
12			The cat in the hat	1	// 1 if search string is empty(!)
13		-	XTC-203-4000	4	// first hyphen
14		3	12345	3	// works with numbers
15					
16					
17					

4.7 TEXTJOIN FUNCTION

With the specified delimiter, the TEXTJOIN function joins values. TEXTJOIN, unlike CONCAT, enables one to choose a list of cells and has an option to overlook empty cells. TEXTJOIN method joins values from 1 or more text strings or text ranges together.

The goal is to combine values by using.

A delimiter. The meaning of the return value.

Formula:

=TEXTJOIN (delimiter, ignore empty, text1, [text2],...)

- **Delimiter:** A character that acts as a separator between two or more texts.
- **Ignore empty:** if empty cells can be ignored or not.
- **text1:** The first attribute or set in text.
- [optional], text2 the 2nd text.

78

One may use TEXTJOIN to join information in cells in the range A1:A3 with the comma and space, as seen below:

=TEXTJOIN (", ",TRUE,A1:A3)

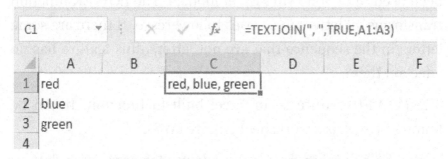

The ignore empty statement governs how empty text/cell values are treated. Empty cells are overlooked if set to true since the delimiter is not replicated in the final result. TEXT JOIN can have empty values in the output if set to false.

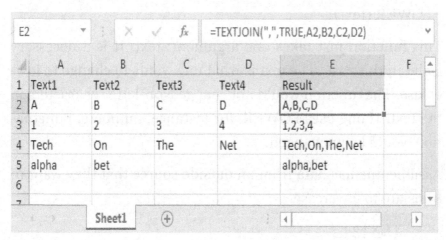

4.8 LOWER FUNCTION

The function will return the lowercase form of the provided text. It was first released in Microsoft Excel 2000 and has since been used in all following Excel models. The LOWER function transforms all letters in a series to lowercase. If there are some letters in the sequence that are not letters, this feature has no effect on them.

The LOWER feature is an Excel built-in function. It can be found in Excel as a worksheet feature (WS).

It may be helpful in financial modeling for organizing data or generating data in a specific format. One may, for example, generate an email account from the names in a data collection.

Formula:

=LOWER (text)

This function just takes one argument: text. It is a necessary claim in this case. The text is what one wants to change to lowercase. The function would not change Non-letter characters in the text. If one uses LOWER, for instance, numbers, punctuation would be unchanged.

Assume one has data from an outside source that they want to translate to lowercase.

- TEXT34
- Text
- Text

The following is a screenshot of the Excel results:

	A	B	C	D
1				
2		LOWER Function		
3				
4		Data	Formula	Result
5		Text	LOWER(B5)	text
6		TEXT34	LOWER(B6)	text34
7		text	LOWER(B7)	text

4.9 UPPER FUNCTION

UPPER function in Excel helps one to transform all text to up-percase.

The UPPER function is an Excel integrated function that is classified as a String or Text Function. It can be found in Excel as the worksheet function (WS).

The UPPER method in MS Excel has the following syntax:

UPPER (text)

BOOK 5
MS Excel Logic's Functions

5.1 AND & OR

The two most common logical functions for checking different parameters are these two functions. The distinction lies about how one goes about doing it:

- AND remains TRUE if all requirements are met; else, FALSE.

- OR remains TRUE if anyone's requirement is met; or else, FALSE.

Although these functions are seldom seen on their own, they are extremely useful when using as part of larger formulas.

Using the function IF formula with inserted AND argument to verify the test outcome in columns B & C and display "Pass" if both are bigger than 70, "Fail" alternatively:

=IF(AND(B2>70, B2>70), "Pass", "Fail")

If only 1 test result is greater than 70 is needed (whether test 1 or test 2), use the OR statement: =IF(OR(B2>70, B2>70), "Pass," "Fail")

=IF(AND(B4>60, C4>60), "Pass", "Fail")

	A	B	C	D
1	Pass if both tests are greater than 60			
2				
3	Item	Test 1	Test 2	Pass / Fail
4	Ava	75	70	Pass
5	Aiden	60	64	Fail
6	Jackson	82	80	Pass
7	Liam	73	75	Pass
8	Sophia	61	58	Fail

=IF(OR(B4>60, C4>60), "Pass", "Fail")

	A	B	C	D
1	Pass if either test is greater than 60			
2				
3	Item	Test 1	Test 2	Pass / Fail
4	Ava	75	70	Pass
5	Aiden	60	64	Pass
6	Jackson	82	80	Pass
7	Liam	73	75	Pass
8	Sophia	61	58	Pass

5.2 IF

When One chooses to sort the data according to a set of logic, the IF feature is often used. The nice thing about the IF formula is that it allows one to use formulas and functions.

Excel will inform whether a certain criterion is satisfied using this formula. One might, for example, want to know which data in column A are greater than four. Using the =IF theorem, Excel will easily auto-generate a "yes" for each cell with a value greater than four and "no" for every cell with a value less than 4.

This is one of the popular formulas.

=IF (logical test, [value if true], [value if false])

Take the following scenario:

=IF (C2 is less than D3, 'TRUE,' 'FALSE')—If the value of C3 is less than the valuation at D3, the condition is true. If the rationale is right, set a cell value to TRUE; otherwise, set it to FALSE.

	A	B	C	D
1	Data		Formula	Answer
2	2		=IF(A2>3,"yes","no")	no
3	2			no
4	5			yes
5	3			no
6	4			yes
7	2			no
8	3			no
9	3			no

=IF (A2 is greater than 3, "Yes," "No")

5.3 MAX & MIN

It is a helpful formula if one has a database with a variety of numbers. One will quickly locate the highest number in the data set with =MAX and the lowest number with =MIN.

=MIN (A2:A9) =MAX (A2:A9)

	A	B	C
1	Data		Formula
2	2		=MAX(A2:A9)
3	2		=MIN(A2:A9)
4	5		
5	3		
6	4		
7	2		
8	3		
9	3		

The MIN and MAX functions assist in determining the maximum and minimum values within a set of values.

=MIN (no.1, [no.2],...)

Such as

- **=MIN (B3:C12):** It will Find the smallest number in all columns B, B2 & column C from B3 to row 12.
- =MAX (no.1, [no.2],...)
- **=MAX (B2:C11):** It will find the highest value between B column & C column from C2 to 11th row in all columns of B & C

SUM | × ✓ fx | =MAX(B2:B11)

	A	B	C
1	**Country**	**Population**	
2	China	1,389,618,778	
3	India	1,311,559,204	
4	USA	331,883,986	
5	Indonesia	264,935,824	
6	Pakistan	210,797,836	
7	Brazil	210,301,591	
8	Nigeria	208,679,114	
9	Bangladesh	161,062,905	
10	Russia	141,944,641	
11	Mexico	127,318,112	
12	**MAX**	=MAX(B2:B11)	**1,389,618,778**
13			

SUM | × ✓ fx | =MIN(B2:B11)

	A	B	C
1	**Country**	**Population**	
2	China	1,389,618,778	
3	India	1,311,559,204	
4	USA	331,883,986	
5	Indonesia	264,935,824	
6	Pakistan	210,797,836	
7	Brazil	210,301,591	
8	Nigeria	208,679,114	
9	Bangladesh	161,062,905	
10	Russia	141,944,641	
11	Mexico	127,318,112	
12	**MIN**	=MIN(B2:B11)	**127,318,112**
13			

5.4 EVEN & ODD

This formula is useful when dealing with data that contains a number of decimals. =EVEN rounding up to the closest even number, whereas =ODD rounding up to the odd closet number. These calculations can round down to the closet odd or even number if one is dealing with negative numbers.

	A	B	C	D	E
1	Data		Formula	Answer - EVEN	Answer - ODD
2	3.2			4	5
3	6.771			8	7
4	4.255			6	5
5	3.1			4	5
6	4.998			6	5
7	7.42			8	9
8	10.112			12	11
9	6.468			8	7

Column D uses the =EVEN method, while column E uses the =ODD method in this case.

For the formula, use =EVEN (SELECT A CELL) & =ODD (SELECT A CELL).

5.5 IFS FUNCTION

This logical IFS Function is in Excel since 2016. The function is an improvement to the Coded IF function, which is far simpler to use. The IFS function tests if 1 or more than one requirement is met or not and consequently returns a value that satisfies the 1st TRUE condition. The Excel IFS function performs several checks and returns the value referring to the first TRUE answer. One can use the IFS function to test several situations without several nested IF statements. IFS makes simpler, easier to understand calculations.

Formula

=IFS (test1, value1, [test2, value2], ...)

Assertions

- Test1 - First rational test.
- Value1 - this is the Result when test1 will be TRUE.
- Test2, value2 - it is [optional] 2nd test & value pair.

5.5.1 RATING FROM HIGHEST TO LOWEST

On a basic scoring scale, the score three or higher is "Good," the score between 2 to 3 is "Avg," and everything below 2 is "Bad." To allocate these values with IFS, three criteria are used: =IFS(A1>=3,"Good",A1>=2,"Avg",A1<2,"Bad")

It's worth noting that in this situation, the parameters are set up to measure higher values first.

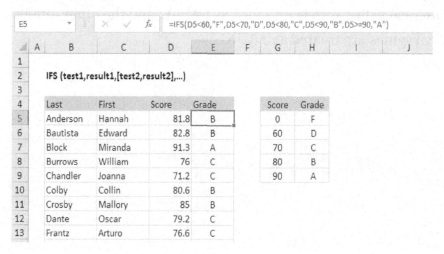

5.6 NOT FUNCTION

This logical NOT function is used to see whether two values are not equal. It will return TRUE if one gives it TRUE and FALSE if one gives it FALSE. As a result, it would still return a logical value in the opposite direction. The NOT function in Excel returns the inverse of a logical value. To reverse a logical value, use the NOT method.

The NOT function is helpful as the financial analyst when one wants to know whether a given criterion was not met

Formula:

=NOT (logical)

Rational (required statement)—The statement must be either logical or numerical. If the specified logical statement is a numerical value, zero is regarded as FALSE, and the other numerical values are treated as TRUE.

BOOK 6
MS Excel Counting Functions

This COUNT function counts the number of cells in a set that only includes numerical data.

=COUNT (value1, [value2],)

Consider the following scenario:

- COUNT (A: A): This function will Counts all quantitative data in column A. To count rows, one must change the range within the formula.
- COUNT (B1:D1): It now has the ability to count rows.

	Clipboard			Font		Allignmen
SUM		× ✓	f_x	=COUNT(B2:B13)		

	A	B	C
1	**Country**	**Population**	
2	China	1,389,618,778	
3	India	1,311,559,204	
4	USA	331,883,986	
5	Indonesia	264,935,824	
6	Pakistan	210,797,836	
7		Empty	Skips non-numerical values
8	Brazil	210,301,591	
9	Nigeria	208,679,114	
10			Skips empty cells
11	Bangladesh	161,062,905	
12	Russia	141,944,641	
13	Mexico	127,318,112	
14	**COUNT**	=COUNT(B2:B13)	Output = 10

6.2 COUNTA

This function, like the COUNT, counts all cells in a specified range. It does, however, count all cells, regardless of their kind. Apart from COUNT, which only counts numerically, this function often counts times, strings, logical values, mistakes, dates, null strings, and text.

=COUNTA (value1, [value2],...)

Such as

COUNTA(42:C13)

It will count rows from 4 to 14 in the C column. Even so, unlike COUNT, one can't count rows using the very same formula. COUNTA (D2:J2), for instance, would count columns D to J Division if one changes the range within the brackets.

6.3 COUNTBLANK

This COUNTBLANK function in Excel counts the number of empty cells in the set.

This is a built-in function that is classified as a Statistical Function.

Formula:

=COUNTBLANK (range)

- To count the number of vacant cells in a range return
- The COUNTBLANK function returns a numeric value.

- This function ignores the cells that contain numbers, errors, text, or other data.

- Formulas that produce a null string ("") would be counted as void, and count blank will count them. The COUNTBLANK function counts the cell as blank, whether it includes a blank text string or the formula that will return a blank text string.

- Cells with a value of 0 are not deemed blank thus will not be counted.

Here is an example for your understanding.

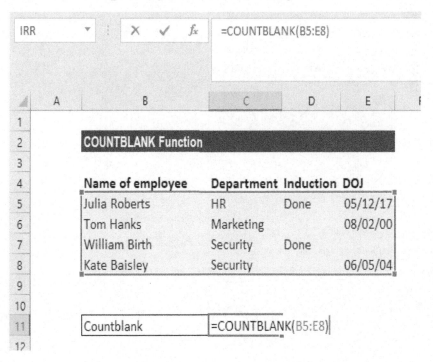

This will give you the result.

| G5 | ▼ | × ✓ _fx_ | =COUNTIF(D5:D12,">100") |

	A	B	C	D	E	F	G	H
1								
2		**COUNTIF (range, criteria)**						
3								
4		Name	State	Sales		Example	Result	
5		Jim	MN	$100.00		Sales over $100	4	
6		Sarah	CA	$125.00		Sales by Jim	3	
7		Jane	GA	$200.00		Sales in California	2	
8		Steve	CA	$50.00				
9		Jim	WY	$75.00				
10		Joan	WA	$150.00				
11		Jane	GA	$200.00				
12		Jim	WY	$50.00				
13								

BOOK 7
Conditional Functions in MS Excel

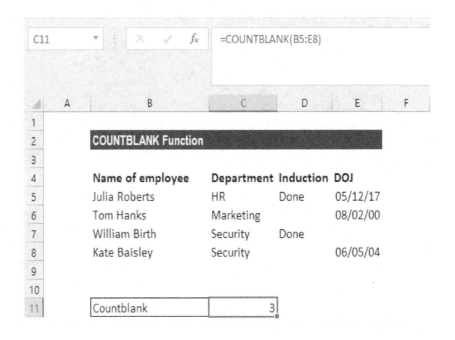

The COUNTIF function is a function that allows one to count the number of cells in a set that satisfies one single requirement. COUNTIF may be used to count the cells with days, amounts, or text in them. For selective matching, COUNTIF's parameters help logical operators (>, <, <>=) & wildcards (? *,). This function is a built-in function. This function is a spreadsheet function that can be used in a formula in a worksheet cell.

Formula:

=COUNTIF (range, criteria)

7.1 AVERAGE

This function is as easy as just getting an average of the no. of the shareholders in the pool of a given company.

=AVERAGE (no.1, [no.2], ...)

Such as

=AVERAGE (B4:B12) – this formula or function shows a very simple average or (SUM (B4:B12)/10)

	A	B	C
		=AVERAGE(B2:B11)	
1	Country	Population	
2	China	1,389,618,778	
3	India	1,311,559,204	
4	USA	331,883,986	
5	Indonesia	264,935,824	
6	Pakistan	210,797,836	
7	Brazil	210,301,591	
8	Nigeria	208,679,114	
9	Bangladesh	161,062,905	
10	Russia	141,944,641	
11	Mexico	127,318,112	
12	**Average**	=AVERAGE(B2:B11)	Output = 435,810,199
13			

7.2 COUNTIFS

This function of Excel calculates the number of cells that satisfy 1 or more parameters. This COUNTIFS may handle parameters dependent on times, amounts, text, and other variables. For selective matching, COUNTIFS accepts logical operators (<>,<,>,=) & wildcards (?,*).

| | fx | =COUNTIFS(C5:C14,"red",D5:D14,"TX") |

	A	B	C	D	E	F	G	H	I	J
1										
2		COUNTIFS function								
3										
4		Date	Color	State	Qty	Total				
5		9-Jan	Red	TX	1	$18.00		Red and TX	3	
6		23-Jan	Blue	CO	2	$34.00				
7		3-Feb	Red	NM	2	$36.00				
8		18-Feb	Blue	TX	1	$17.00				
9		2-Mar	Blue	AZ	3	$51.00				
10		15-Mar	Red	AZ	1	$17.00				
11		25-Mar	Red	TX	2	$36.00				
12		2-Apr	Red	CO	4	$72.00				
13		12-Apr	Blue	AZ	2	$34.00				
14		30-Apr	Red	TX	3	$54.00				
15										
16										

The COUNTIFS function has the following syntax:

=COUNTIFS (range One, criteria One, [range Two, criteria Two,... range n, criteria n])

Parameters:

- 1st range: Criteria1 can be applied to a cells' range
- 1st criterion: The standards that are used to decide which cells will be included in the result.
- Range1 is contrasted with criteria1, Range 2, to range n,... It's an option. It's the collection of cells on which one would want to add criteria2,... criteria n. A total of 127 ranges are possible.

- Criteria2, to criteria n: It's optional. It's used to figure out which cells will be included in the result. Criteria 2 is extended against range 2, Criteria 3 is extended against range 3, and so forth. There are a total of 127 parameters that can be included.
- Return: The COUNTIFS operation returns a numeric value.

7.3 SUMIFS FUNCTION

This SUMIFS function in Excel adds all numbers in the set of cells depending on one or more parameters.

This function is a Math Function that is used in Excel and can be used as part of a formula. When neighboring cells satisfy conditions dependent on times, numbers, or code, SUMIFS may be used to sum values. For selective matching, SUMIFS accepts logical operators (>,><,=) & wildcards (?,*,).

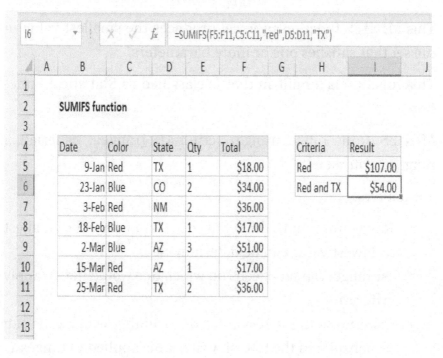

Formula:

=SUMIFS (sum range, range1, criteria1, [range2], [criteria2],...)

Parameters:

- Sum range - The number to be added together.
- Range1 - Evaluate the first range.
- Criteria1 - The criterion that will be applied to range 1.
- It is an optional range2, the 2nd range to consider.
- Second criterion - [optional] The criterion that will be applied to range 2.

7.4 MINIFS FUNCTION

This MINIFS function in Excel produces the smallest value in the set that satisfies one or more parameters.

This function is a built-in that is classified as Statistical Function.

MINIFS (min range, range1, criteria1, [range2, criteria2,... range n, criteria n])

Parameters:

- Range minimum: the set of cells from which the smallest or lowest value can be determined.
- 1st range: the set of cells on which one would like to apply criteria1.
- Criteria1 is the criterion for determining which cells can be considered the lowest. Criteria1 is applied to ranges 1.

- Range 2 to range n–It's the collection of cells on which one would want to add criteria2 to criteria n. A total of 126 ranges are possible.
- Criteria2, to criteria n: It's used to figure out which cells can be considered the smallest. Criteria 2 is extended to range 2, Criteria 3 is applied to range 3, and so forth. There are a total of 126 parameters that can be included.
- Results: Provided 1 or more parameters, this function results in a numeric value that reflects the smallest value in the number of cells.

	A	B	C	D	E	F
E2			f_x	=MINIFS(C2:C9,A2:A9,"Group A")		
1	Golf Team	Player	Score		Min for Group A	
2	Group A	Jonathan	72		69	
3	Group A	Jane	69			
4	Group A	Sarah	103		Min for Group B (over 0)	
5	Group A	Ethan	102		75	
6	Group B	Samantha	78			
7	Group B	Gary	0		Min for Players starting with S	
8	Group B	Henry	75		78	
9	Group B	Fred	81			
10						
11						

Sheet1

7.5 AVERAGEIF

This AVERAGEIF function in MS Excel calculates the average of all quantities in a series of cells based on a set of parameters. It calculates the numbers' average in a set that satisfies defined requirements.

For partial matching, AVERAGEIF parameters may involve logical operators (>,>,<=) & wildcards (*,?).

BOOK 8
MS Excel Functions of Date & Time

Formula:

The AVERAGEIFS function in Excel has the following syntax:

=AVERAGEIFS (average range, criteria1 range, criteria1, [criteria2 range, criteria2, criteria3 range, criteria3,...])

Parameters:

- The average range is a term that refers to the set of cells one would like to average.
- Criteria1 range, Criteria2 range are the set against which the associated parameters would be applied. There can be as many as 127 categories of standards.
- Criteria 1, Criteria 2, this criterion will be applied against the corresponding set. As a result, criteria1 is assigned to criteria1 range, criteria 2 to criteria 2 range, and so on.

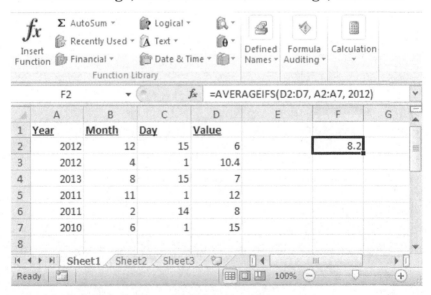

It's possible that one needs to timestamp a worksheet any time it's accessed.

◢	A	B	C
1		Today's Date:	
2		1/9/2019	
3			
4	Data		Formula
5	2		=SUM(A2:A9)
6	2		=SUM(A2,A9)
7	5		=SUM(A2:A9)/5
8	3		

Rather than manually entering the date, use =TODAY (). That's correct, one doesn't even need to add any value in the brackets, and the worksheet will automatically refresh with the present date any time it's accessed.

To add the present date, time in a cell, use the

=NOW () function.

The simplicity of this function is that they don't need any assertions; one simply types the formulas as specified.

◢	A	B	C
1	Today's date	Wednesday, May 24, 2017	=TODAY()
2	Current date & time	05/24/2017 14:30	=NOW()

=EOMONTH will be utilized to find the ongoing month's last day, as well as future months' last days. Using =EOMONTH in-stead of switching between calendars and between a schedule and the spreadsheet (START DATE, 0). Take the formula a little forward and apply

Formula:

=EOMONTH (start-date, 1) to it to determine the next month.

In this case, notice how the amount at the end of the calculation can be increased to approximate future months.

Another note regarding this calculation: when inserting the start date, make sure to use the DATE feature (2018, 3, 21), which is March 21, 2018, because the formula can operate right now. If the method returns a #NUM! Mistake, the date is most likely incorrectly formatted.

8.3 DATEDIF

This function estimates the number of days, months, years be-tween 2 dates. The DATEDIF function of Excel calculates the difference in days, years, or months between specified dates. The DATEDIF (Date plus sign Dive) function arises from Lotus 1-2-3 and is a "compatibility" function.

A number that represents the amount of time that has passed between 2 dates has such a formula.

=DATEDIF (start date, end date, unit)

Parameters:

- The start date is in Excel date number format, and this is the start date.

- The end date is the end date in excel format.

- Unit is the time variable that would be used (days, years, or months).

Unit	Outcome
md	Calculates in days, overlooking months & years
y	Calculates in years
yd	Calculates in days, overlooking years
m	Calculates in months
d	Calculates in days
ym	Calculates in months, overlooking years

E5	▾	:	✕	✓	*fx*	=DATEDIF(B5,C5,"y")		

▲	A	B	C	D	E	F	G
1							
2		DATEDIF (start, end, unit)					
3							
4		Start date	End date	Unit	Result	Notes	
5		1-Jan-18	1-Mar-20	Y	2	Difference in complete years	
6		1-Jan-18	1-Mar-20	M	26	Difference in complete months	
7		1-Jan-18	1-Mar-20	D	790	Difference in days	
8		1-Jan-18	1-Mar-20	MD	0	Difference in days, ignoring months and years	
9		1-Jan-18	1-Mar-20	YM	2	Difference in months, ignoring days and years	
10		1-Jan-18	1-Mar-20	YD	59	Difference in days, ignoring years	
11							
12							
13							

8.4 WORKDAY FUNCTION

Depending on an equivalent value one provides with the function, this WORKDAY function takes the date and returns the closest working day in the past or future. This function can be used to measure things like ship times, arrival dates, and end dates that include working or non-working days to be taken into consideration.

Formula:

=WORKDAY (start date, days, [holidays])

Parameters:

- The start date is the date, to begin with.
- Days are the number of working days prior to or after the beginning date.
- Holidays it is optional, and the following is a list of dates that can be called non-working days. One will find the number of workdays between 2 dates using this

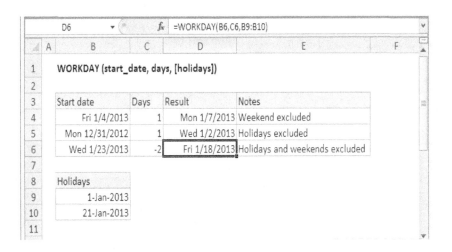

8.5 NETWORKDAYS

One will find the number of workdays between 2 dates using this NETWORKDAYS function. The WORKDAY function in Excel has the following formula:

=WORKDAY (start_date, days, [weekend], [holidays])

- The first 2 parameters, similar to WORKDAY's, are needed:
- The start date is the beginning date.

112

- Days are the number of working days prior to (- value) or after (+ value) the beginning date. The days' statement is shortened to an integer if it is provided as the decimal number.
- The final 2 parameters are not mandatory:
- Weekend determines which weekdays can be considered as weekends. As seen below, this may be a number or a series.

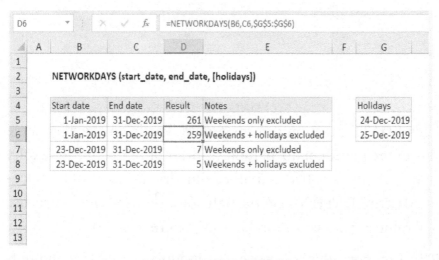

8.6 DATE FUNCTION

This DATE function generates a correct date by combining the components of the day, year, and month.

The DATE feature is important for putting together dates that need to adjust dynamically depending on certain worksheet values.

Formula:

=DATE (year, month, day)

- The year is represented by a number.
- The month is shown by a number.

- Day is the number of days.

	A	B	C	D	E	F	G	H
1								
2		DATE (year,month,day)						
3								
4		Year	Month	Day	Result			
5		2019	1	1	1-Jan-19			
6		2019	1	5	5-Jan-19			
7		2019	2	15	15-Feb-19			
8		2019	1	60	1-Mar-19			
9		2019	36	1	1-Dec-21			
10		2019	1	-1	30-Dec-18			
11								
12								
13								

8.7 EDATE FUNCTION

This EDATE function returns a date that is on the very same day of the month, n no. of months prior or in the future. Expiry dates, maturity dates, and other time frames may all be calculated with EDATE. To get the date for months in the future, use a + value and a - value for dates in the previous time.

This function adds a given no. of months to the date and outputs a serial date as the effect.

The EDATE role assists a financial analyst in estimating overview counts by month as well as calculating maturity dates for the business payable and receivable that come on the last day of the month.

=EDATE (start date, months)

Parameters:

- The start date is the beginning date in Excel format.
- Months: The number of months prior to or after the beginning date.

One may use EDATE like this if A1 includes the date February 1, 2018:

=EDATE(A1, 2) // outcomes April 1, 2018

=EDATE(A1, 4) // outcomes June 1, 2018

=EDATE(A1,-2) // outcomes December 1, 2018

=EDATE(A1,-3) // outcomes November 1, 2017

8.8 WEEKDAY FUNCTION

This WEEKDAY function takes one date and gives a number from 1 to 7 that defines the weekday. WEEKDAY returns 1 is Sunday, and 7 is Saturday by default. The WEEKDAY feature may be used with other formulas to verify the day of the week and respond accordingly.

Formula:

=WEEKDAY (serial number, [return type])

Parameters:

- The serial number is the date for which the day of the week is desired.
- The return type is optional. It is A number that represents the weekday mapping scheme. The default value is 1.

BOOK 9
Excel Problems & Their Solutions

9.1 COPY THE FORMULA

To easily copy a formula, use the following steps:

- Hovering over a cell with the formula in the bottom-right corner (one will see that the pointer has become a thick black +)

- Press the black + sign twice.

- Taking formulas or Values and Pasting Them.

- If this technique doesn't fit because the range starts at a blank cell and ends at a blank cell, or one does not want to pull a formula down to Thousand rows, do this instead:

- Select the first cell one want to copy or fill in with data.

- In the name box, write the address of the last cell in the range where one wants to enter the data or the formula, then press Shift + Enter.

- To modify the formula in the first cell, press F2.

- Finally, press Ctrl + Enter.

9.2 FILL IN THE CELLS RAPIDLY

In 2013, Excel became self-aware. Let's say one has 2 columns of names and needs to generate email addresses from both of them. Simply do that for the 1st row, and Excel will figure out what the user is talking about and complete the rest for them. This was feasible prior to 2013, but it required the use of certain methods (FIND, LEFT, etc.). Now, this is even smoother and can impress people. If Flash Fill is switched (File Options Advanced), it can just start running when one types. Or get it running manually by pressing Data, then select Flash Fill or Ctrl E.

9.2.1 TOTAL A ROW OR A COLUMN

To rapidly total a row or a column, in the last cell, press Alt + =

9.2.2 DELETE DOUBLE ROWS

To remove rows with redundant results, follow these instructions:

Choose the information range to be de-duplicated generally Ctrl + A will suffice. Select the Data menu option from the menu ribbon.

9.3 CHOOSE TO REMOVE DUPLICATES KEY

Choose if the range has a header row.

Click OK

9.3.1 FILTERS

Quickly examine data in the table. Filtering essentially masks non-interesting results. Filters can usually pull out a certain attribute (for example, red cars) and cover the rest. Although in more recent implementations of Excel, one can also even filter on no. values—for example, is greater than, highest 10 percent, etc., and the color of the cell. Filtering becomes more efficient as one needs to scan more than 1 column in combination—for example, all colors and cars to identify the red car. Alt D F F is the shortcut—Simpler than it seems, gives it a try.

Variable Formatting and Sorting are also used for the same thing. Sorting necessitates rearranging the list, which may be inconvenient and undesirable. Representation is made possible through conditional formatting. Filtering is a quick and efficient process. Make wise decisions.

9.3.2 COPY THE VALUES

Using the following keyboard shortcut series to copy just values and not the formulas:

- To pick the entire range of data, press Ctrl + A (or select the range with the help of the cursor)

- To copy the files, press Ctrl + C.

- As one arrives at their goal, click Alt + E, then S, press V, and finally Enter.

- Ctrl + A > Ctrl + C >Alt + E S, V > Enter is the complete list.

- If one practices this a few times and does it in front of the superiors, they will undoubtedly be in appreciation of the latest skills.

9.4 IMPORT A TABLE FROM THE INTERNET

One will frequently need to download data from the web and wish there was a simpler way. So, there's one choice. Let's presume one wants to import the record of baseball history a home run hitter from the baseball archive. To see this information in an Excel file, simply follow these steps:

- From the ribbon, choose the Data menu selection.

- Choose from the Web.

- Type http://www.****** into the window bar of the browser.

- In the browser window, press the Go icon.

- Roll down to the home (table) run chart.

- Delete the already selected row (s)

Take these two measures to remove the current row easily.

- Press Shift + Space to select the row(s).

- Using Ctrl + -, remove the selected row(s).

- Current Column that needs to be removed (s)

Follow these steps to delete the present column(s) swiftly.

- Pick the column by Ctrl + Space.

- Erase the picked column by Ctrl + minus sign.

9.5 FAST AGGREGATION

Quick Tool includes aggregate stats, such as Count, Average, Max, Min, Numerical Count, and Amount of the data from a chosen set without entering any algorithm. To display these stats in the toolbar on the bottom right, click on the toolbar and select the appropriate statistic.

- Click on to pick the table check box.

- Choose Import.

- Click OK

9.6 IFERROR

When the formula produces a mistake, the Excel IFERROR feature returns a custom outcome, and when no error is found, it returns a normal result. IFERROR is a simple way to catch and handle errors without the need for nested IF statements.

Formula:

=IFERROR (value, value if error)

Parameters:

- Value is the value, or algorithm or reference, that would be used to look for errors.
- Value iferror is the value to the outcome if a mistake is present.

When an error is found in a calculation, the IFERROR algorithm "catches" the error and returns an alternate answer or formula.

The IFERROR module may be used to catch and treat errors caused by other functions or formulas. The following errors are detected by IFERROR: #REF!, #DIV/0!, #VALUE!, #NUM!, #NULL! Or #NAME?

If A1 includes 10, B1 is empty, and C1 includes the formula =A1/B1, this iferror will catch the mistake #DIV/0 that is caused by dividing A1/B1.

=IFERROR (A1/B1, please fill in the blanks in B1")

If B1 is null or void, C1 will show the message "Please insert a value in B1" as long as B1 is empty. The formula would return the product of A1/B1 when a number is inserted in B1.

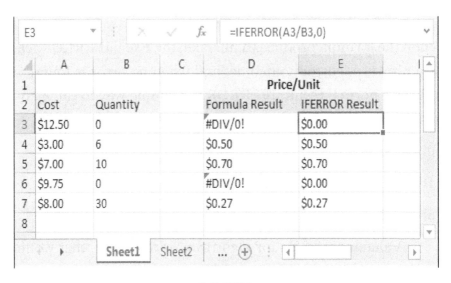

E3			f_x	=IFERROR(A3/B3,0)		
	A	B	C	D	E	
1					Price/Unit	
2	Cost	Quantity		Formula Result	IFERROR Result	
3	$12.50	0		#DIV/0!	$0.00	
4	$3.00	6		$0.50	$0.50	
5	$7.00	10		$0.70	$0.70	
6	$9.75	0		#DIV/0!	$0.00	
7	$8.00	30		$0.27	$0.27	
8						

Sheet1 Sheet2 ...

9.7 IFNA

When the formula produces a #N/A error, the IFNA function displays the customized result, and when no mistake is found, it returns a normal outcome.

IFNA is a clever way to capture and treat #N/A errors when ignoring any other errors.

Formula:

=IFNA (value, value_if_na)

Parameters:

- Value is the value, algorithm, or reference that would be used to look for errors.
- Value ifna is if there is a #N/A mistake, this will be the value to be returned.

The following is an illustration of IFNA being used to capture #N/A errors with VLOOKUP:

=IFNA (VLOOKUP(A1,table,2,0),"Not found")

124

- When a value is blank, it is treated as a blank string ("") rather than a mistake.
- If the ifna value is set to a blank string (""), when a mistake occurs, no message is shown.

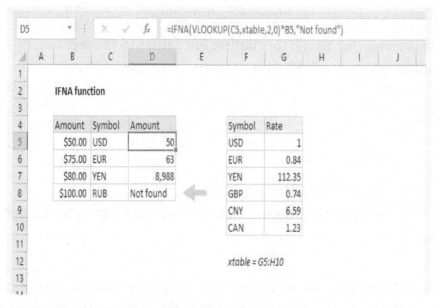

9.8 FORMULAS NOT WORKING

It's possible that when one confirms a formula (by pressing enter), the answer doesn't appear; rather,

The formula is shown in the cell.

Number 1	40
Number 2	50

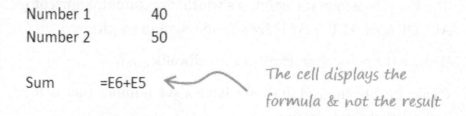

The Solution is:

The issue is that the cell is formatted as text, so Excel interprets the formula as text.

Simply transform the cell to a Number/ General format, then verify the formula.

This occurs more often by chance when the spreadsheet displays all calculations but not their output.

This is not due to cell formatting but rather to the fact that one might have moved the formula view by pressing Ctrl ~

	1	=C4+1	=D4+1
Sales	100	200	250
Commission	=C5*10%	=D5*10%	=E5*10%

The entire spreadsheet is showing formulas & not the result

The Solution is to simply click Ctrl ~ again to return to regular mode.

Sometimes the cells would be loaded up with hashes. This may be because the cell data does not fit in the cell's width. The number or data is in excess of 253 letters.

A -ve number in the cell has been configured as a Date or Time format. Note the date or time must be positive numbers.

The Fix is to widen the column's width. For autofit, Shortcut is ALT OCA, or ALT OCW is for specific custom width)

Reduce the no of characters in the cell value.

Please ensure the cell does not have a -ve number that is formatted as the date or time.

9.11 PAGE BREAKS

Page breaks are innocuous, and they make the spreadsheet untidy.

The Solution is to Go to Options, then to Advanced, then to Scroll down to look for displaying options for the current spreadsheet, then untick Page Breaks.

9.12 EXCEL SECURITY

It is possible to apply encryption to Excel spreadsheets, but it is riddled with issues. The focus of protection is on the spreadsheet's configuration rather than the details. One may attempt to lock certain sheets and cells to prevent users from modifying the layout & formula, but they can generally alter any or all of it if one can see the data. So, protect your work by:

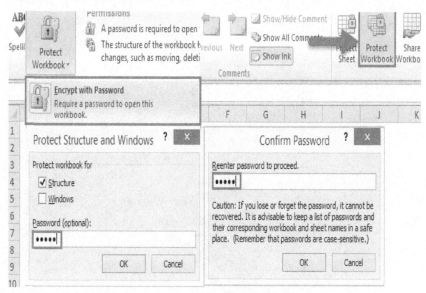

Take a tour

Welcome to Excel

Blank workbook

C D

7
8
9
10

TASK LIST
MY TASKS
START DATE
DUE DATE

Total a List

Cost

$22.00

$102.00

$15.00

Total $139.00

Item
Item
Item
Item

Total a List

Shared

BOOK 10
Pivot Table in MS Excel

A Pivot Table is a tool for summarizing, sorting, reorganizing, grouping, counting, totaling, or averaging data in the table. It helps one to change rows into columns and columns into rows. It helps one group the data by some area (column) and do advanced calculations on it. One of Excel's most useful functionality is pivot tables. You may use a pivot table to derive the meaning from a huge, complex data collection.

10.1 WHY ARE PIVOT TABLES IMPORTANT?

In a database, pivot tables are being used to reorganize information. Pivot tables will not change the details, so based on what one wants them to do, they will add up values and evaluate various data in the spreadsheet.

Pivot tables are used to summarize data and to locate specific values in a sector. This is an easy way to see all of the value in the sector, as well as identify typos and other discrepancies. A PivotTable is a versatile tool for calculating, summarizing, and analyzing results, allowing one to see similarities, patterns, and trends.

Let's start with this example. For example, how many people are in a fraternity house? One may think they do not have a lot of info, but it will be helpful with larger datasets.

Select Data, then go to Pivot Table to build the Pivot Table. Excel can fill the Pivot Table instinctively, but one can still rearrange the files. And they have a choice of four choices.

Report Filter: This feature helps one to see only specific rows in the data. For e.g., instead of including all people in the filter, one might choose only to include a certain fraternity.

- Column Labels: This may be the dataset's headers.

- Row Labels: This may be the data's rows. Data from the columns can be moved to both a Row & Column labels.

- Value: This segment encourages one to take a different approach to the results. One can total, list, average, avg, min, count amounts, and do a couple of other maneuverings for the data instead of only taking in some statistical value. In truth, when one moves a field to Value, it does a count.

This Excel method is used to do data analysis without the use of formulas. It is simple to do, which takes less time.

- To make a pivot table, go to the Insert tab and choose the PivotTable key. A dialogue box appears on the screen. Check the information and then press OK.

- The necessary data will appear in the form of the pivot table after one drags the requisite amount of fields.

10.2 CREATING PIVOT TABLES

Follow the measures below to add a pivot table.

- Choose needed cells inside the data collection by selecting them.

- Choose PivotTable from the Tables group on the Insert tab.

The dialogue box below occurs. Excel can choose the data for everyone automatically. The current Worksheet is the default position for the new pivot table.

Choose OK.

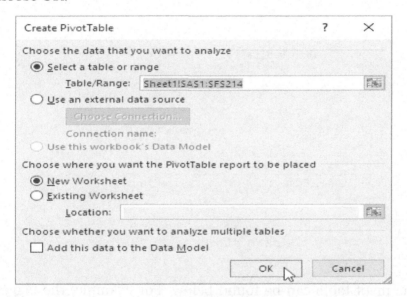

10.2.1 DRAG FIELDS

The Fields pane for PivotTables occurs. Drag the fields to the various areas to get the cumulative sum exported for each commodity.

- To the Rows area, add the Product field.

- To the Values area, add the Amount field.

- To the Filters section, add the Country area.

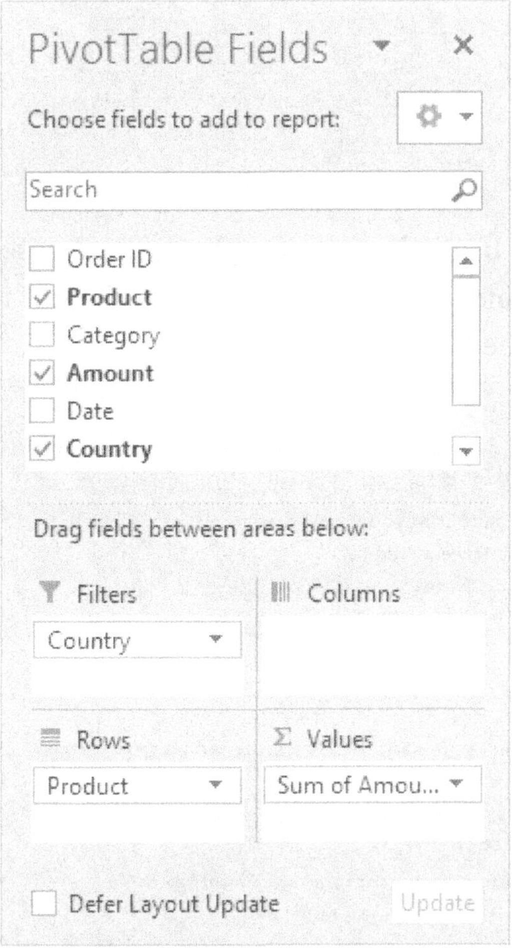

PivotTable Fields ▼ ✕

Choose fields to add to report: ⚙ ▼

Search 🔍

☐ Order ID
☑ **Product**
☐ Category
☑ **Amount**
☐ Date
☑ **Country**

Drag fields between areas below:

▼ Filters | ⊪ Columns
Country ▼ |

≡ Rows | Σ Values
Product ▼ | Sum of Amou... ▼

☐ Defer Layout Update | Update

The pivot table can be found below. For example, the biggest export item is bananas. That's how simple pivot tables are.

	A	B	C
1	Country	(All) ▼	
2			
3	Row Labels ▼	Sum of Amount	
4	Apple	191257	
5	Banana	340295	
6	Beans	57281	
7	Broccoli	142439	
8	Carrots	136945	
9	Mango	57079	
10	Orange	104438	
11	**Grand Total**	**1029734**	
12			

10.2.2 SORTING

Sort a pivot table to put Bananas at the top of the table select any cell in the column (Sum of Amount) can by clicking it.

Sort Largest to Smallest by right-clicking and selecting Sort.

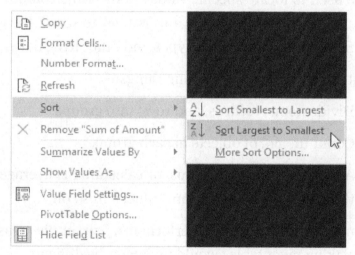

Outcome

	A	B	C
1	Country	(All) ▼	
2			
3	Row Labels ↵	Sum of Amount	
4	Banana	340295	
5	Apple	191257	
6	Broccoli	142439	
7	Carrots	136945	
8	Orange	104438	
9	Beans	57281	
10	Mango	57079	
11	**Grand Total**	**1029734**	
12			

10.3 PRACTICAL EXAMPLES OF A PIVOT TABLE

Create a set of unique values using a pivot table. Pivot tables may be used to locate specific values in the table column since they summarize results. This is an easy way to see all the values in the field, as well as identify typos and other irregularities.

A pivot table will do the following things:

- Divide items, records, and rows into groups.

- Count the no. of objects in each group.

- Add the worth of the items, or calculate the average, find the minimum or maximum value, and so on.

One can see how pivot tables perform in a few simple measures. Then making pivot tables would no longer be difficult.

Select the dataset by clicking on it.

CUSTOMER	REGION	ORDER DATE	SALES	MONTH	YEAR
Acme, inc.	NORTH	13/04/2014	$24,640	April	2014
Widget Corp	SOUTH	21/12/2014	$24,040	December	2014
123 Warehousing	EAST	15/02/2014	$29,923	February	2014
Demo Company	WEST	14/05/2014	$66,901	May	2014
Smith and Co.	NORTH	28/06/2015	$63,116	June	2015
Foo Bars	SOUTH	15/01/2015	$38,281	January	2015
ABC Telecom	EAST	22/08/2015	$57,650	August	2015
Fake Brothers	WEST	31/12/2015	$90,967	December	2015

Go to *Insert then Pivot Table*

Add the Pivot Table in the **New or previous Worksheet**

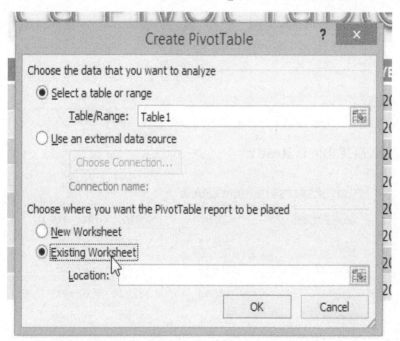

Drag & Change the Fields

The Pivot Table is Ready

Sum of SALES	Column Labels		
Row Labels	2014	2015	Grand Total
EAST	29923	57650	87573
NORTH	24640	63116	87756
SOUTH	24640	38281	62921
WEST	66901	90967	157868
Grand Total	146104	250014	396118

When one has entered all of the details, they need in the Excel sheet, sort it in a way to make it easy to process when converted to a pivot table.

To filter the files, go to the top navigation bar and press the "Data" button, then the "Sort" button. One may choose to organize the data through a column and in any order. Select the column title under "Column" to organize the spreadsheet by "Views to Date," for instance, and then choose whether to order the articles from smallest to largest or vice versa.

Select "OK" in the Sort bottom-right window's corner to rearrange every row of the sheet by the number of views every blog post has obtained.

10.5 DRAG & DROP A FIELD IN THE AREA OF "ROW LABELS"

Excel can build a pivot table after one has ordered it to make the pivot table. The next move is to drag, drop the field in the "Row Labels" area, labeled with the names of columns in the spreadsheet. This will decide which specific identification the pivot table will use to organize the data (e.g., blog post title, or product name, etc.).

Consider the following scenario: one wants to arrange a large amount of posting data by post title. Simply press and drag the "Title" region to the "Row Labels" section to accomplish this.

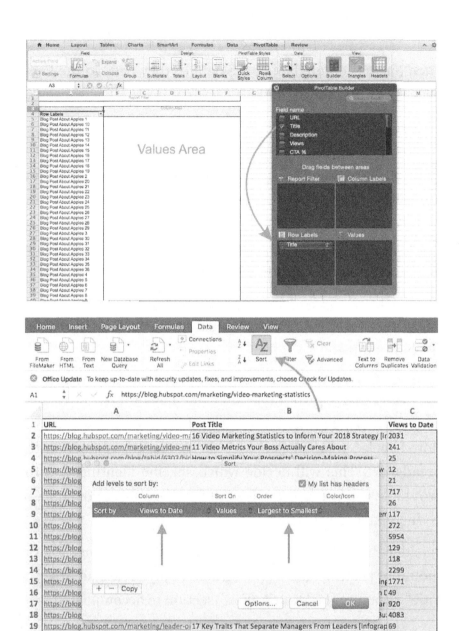

The sum of a given amount would be determined by standard, but based on whether one chooses to quantify, they can easily adjust this to anything like median, maxi, or mini. On Mac, pick the options one wants by clicking on the small I next to the value in the "Values" field, then clicking "OK." Once one has made their choice, the pivot table will be revised to reflect it.

To enter the menu on a PC, click on the tiny upside-down triangle next to the value and choose "Value Field Settings."

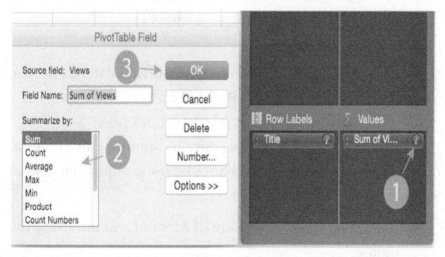

10.7 FILTERING

For instance, if one applies the filter on this pivot table by Country since one added the Country field to the Filters area. What products, for example, can one sell the most to Paris?

Pick Paris/France from the filter drop-down menu.

As a result, the primary export to Paris is apples.

	A	B	C
1	Country	France ⠆	
2			
3	Row Labels ⠆	Sum of Amount	
4	Apple	80193	
5	Banana	36094	
6	Carrots	9104	
7	Mango	7388	
8	Broccoli	5341	
9	Orange	2256	
10	Beans	680	
11	Grand Total	141056	
12			

Remember: To just see the numbers of individual items, use the regular filter (triangle next to Row Labels).

10.8 CHANGE SUMMARY CALCULATION

Excel sums up the data by necessity by summing or counting the products. Conduct the measures below to adjust the kind of formula one chooses to use.

- Choose any cell in the Sum of Amount column using the mouse.

- Choose Value Field Settings from the context menu by right-clicking.

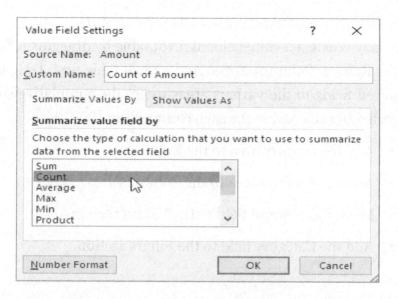

- 3. Decide on the kind of equation one will use. Click Count, for instance.

- 4. Choose OK.

As a result, 'Apple' instructions accounted for 16 of the 28 orders sent to France.

	A	B	C
1	Country	France 🔽	
2			
3	**Row Labels** 🔽	**Count of Amount**	
4	Apple	16	
5	Banana	7	
6	Carrots	1	
7	Mango	1	
8	Orange	1	
9	Beans	1	
10	Broccoli	1	
11	**Grand Total**	28	
12			

One may create a 2-dimensional pivot table by dragging a field to the Rows & Columns areas. Add a pivot table first. Drag the required fields to the various areas to get the cumulative sum exported to each nation for each commodity.

- Add the country area to the Rows.

- Add the Product area to the Columns area.

- Move the Amount field to the Values section.

- Add the Category field to the Filters section.

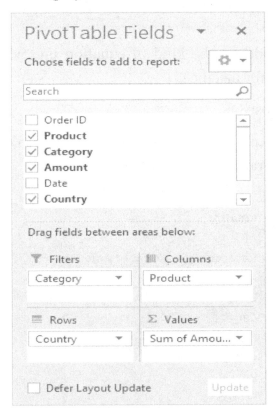

The 2-dimensional pivot table can be seen below.

	A	B	C	D	E	F	G	H	I	J
1	Category	(All)								
2										
3	Sum of Amount	Column								
4	Row Labels	Apple	Banana	Beans	Broccoli	Carrots	Mango	Orange	Grand Total	
5	Australia	20634	52721	14433	17953	8106	9186	8680	131713	
6	Canada	24867	33775		12407		3767	19929	94745	
7	France	80193	36094	680	5341	9104	7388	2256	141056	
8	Germany	9082	39686	29905	37197	21636	8775	8887	155168	
9	New Zealand	10332	40050		4390			12010	66782	
10	United Kingdom	17534	42908	5100	38436	41815	5600	21744	173137	
11	United States	28615	95061	7163	26715	56284	22363	30932	267133	
12	Grand Total	191257	340295	57281	142439	136945	57079	104438	1029734	
13										

Build a pivot chart and add a filter to conveniently compare these figures. Perhaps this is a move too far for a beginner, but it demonstrates one of Excel's many other useful pivot table functions.

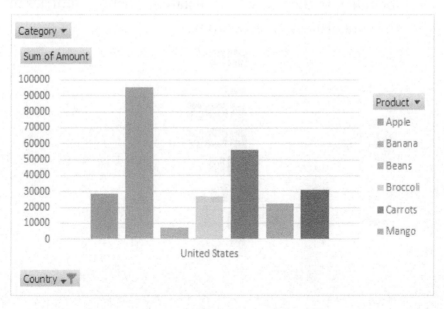

10.9.1 NEW AI FEATURES IN EXCEL

- Bid farewell to data entry with the addition of new image processing features. Just select a screenshot via the app of Excel Android app, and the image will be instantly converted into a completely editable table.

- Insights powered by AI that are based on ideas.

- Tapping the bolt symbol reveals hidden phenomena, patterns, as well as other outliers in a matter of seconds, speeding up the decision-making phase.

- New Data Forms

- Excel will also comprehend real-world topics such as geography and stocks—Converts plain text into layers of immersive data. One can pull position-sensitive data and include it in the study by translating a list of countries in the spreadsheet for geography.

Select entire pivot table	Ctrl A	⌘ A
Toggle pivot table field checkbox	Space	Space
Group pivot table items	Alt Shift →	⌘ ⇧ K
Ungroup pivot table items	Alt Shift ←	⌘ ⇧ J
Hide pivot table item	Ctrl -	Ctrl -
Create pivot chart on same worksheet	Alt F1	
Create pivot chart on new worksheet	F11	Fn F11
Open pivot table wizard	Alt D P	⌘ ⌥ P

BOOK 11
Charts & Graphs with Microsoft Excel

A macro is a sequence of acts or an equation that can be used or repeated several times. By recording or saving the input patterns, such as cursor strokes or keyboard clicks, a macro aids in computerizing or repeated functions. Once this information is saved, it is used to create a macro that is accessible to all updates.

- Macros help by saving time by recording, storing, and running routine tasks when needed.

- Macros can be found in the display tab. Tap on macros to record the macro.

- Then choose the choice to record macros.

- Pay attention. Anything one does with the spreadsheet is now recordered.

- Press the stop recording choice that occurs when one clicks the macros icon to stop recording.

Charts and graphs help one to make sense of the infor-mation by simply visualizing numeric values. In presen-tations, charts & graphs are often used to provide a brief snapshot of development or outcomes to management, clients, or team members. One can make a chart or graph to display almost every kind of quantitative data, saving them the time and effort of sifting through databases to identify relationships and patterns.

Excel makes it simple to produce charts and graphs, par-ticularly when one can store the data in the Excel spread-sheet rather than importing it from another application. Excel also comes with a number of pre-made charts and graph formats from which one can choose that better re-flects the data relationship they want to emphasize. When one has a ton of numeric details on the worksheet, they will use a chart, graph to help make sense of it. Excel has a number of chart formats, each of which is well adapted to a certain form of data processing.

11.1 ONE MUST THINK IS CHART AND GRAPH ARE THE SAME THIN-GS?

On a technical level? No, they refer to different things, and the words are unrelated.

In the modern world? Yes, they're interchangeable, and most people accept both of them. Despite the fact that the terms are frequently used synonymously, they are unique. Graphs are the simplest graphic representation of numbers, and they usually show data point value over time. Charts are more complicated since they help to equate parts of the data set to other data of the same collection. Charts are also more appealing than graphs because they often have a distinct shape from a standard x- & y-axis.

11.2 CHARTS IN EXCEL

A chart is a representation of data in both columns & rows in a visual format. Charts are often used to evaluate data sets for trends and patterns. Assume one has been keeping track of revenue data in Excel for the last 3 years. They will clearly see which year had the most revenue and which year had the lowest when looking at charts. One may also use charts to equate defined goals to real accomplishments. Graphs are also thought to be more aesthetically appealing than graphs. A pie chart, for instance, is used to show the relative share of a given section of the data collection compared to other segments present.

If one chooses to present the % contributions of the various categories of activities that make up a 40-hour work /week for workers in the company instead of the adjustments in hours worked with annual leaves over 5 years, one should definitely add a pie chart into the spreadsheet for the desired result.

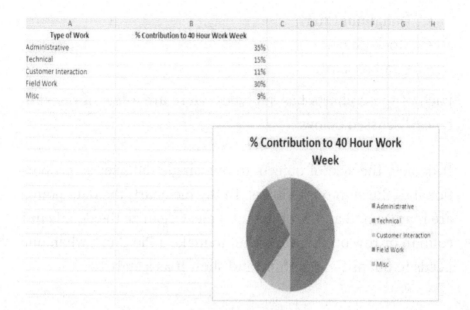

	A	B	C	D	E	F	G	H
	Type of Work	% Contribution to 40 Hour Work Week						
	Administrative	35%						
	Technical	15%						
	Customer Interaction	11%						
	Field Work	30%						
	Misc	9%						

11.3 TYPES OF CHARTS

Various situations require various chart forms. Excel has a variety of chart formats that one can use. The form of chart one chooses is determined by the data one wants to represent. Excel 2013 and later versions have a feature that analyses the data and recommends the chart forms one can use, making it easier for consumers.

The key chart forms available in Excel are as follows:

- Surface Chart.
- Line Chart.
- XY (Scatter) Chart.
- Pie Chart.
- Radar Chart.
- Column Chart.
- Bar Chart.
- Area Chart.
- Bubble Chart.

151

- Doughnut Chart.
- Stock Chart.
- Combo Chart.

Each of these charts has subtypes. Here are a few of the subtypes discussed below.

11.3.1 PIE CHARTS

It depicts the size of objects in one single data set as proportional to the sum of the items. In the pie chart, the data points are represented as a % of the total pie. Organize the details in 1 column or row on the worksheet to make a Pie Chart when one needs to quantify something and show it as a statistic.

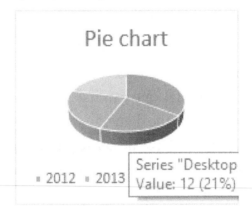

11.3.2 DOUGHNUT CHART

It reveals the connection of pieces to the whole. It is identical to the Pie Chart, with the main exception that a Doughnut Chart can include more than 1 data set. However, the Pie Chart can include only 1 data series.

A Doughnut Chart includes circles with each ring indicates 1 data set. To construct a Doughnut Chart, place the data in columns or rows on the spreadsheet.

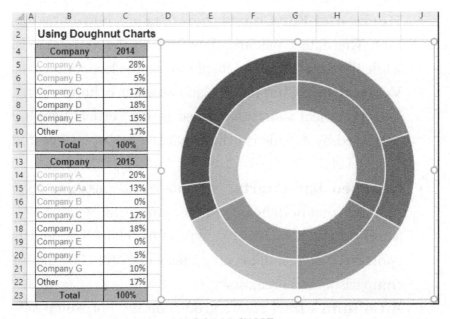

	A	B	C
2		**Using Doughnut Charts**	
4		Company	2014
5		Company A	28%
6		Company B	5%
7		Company C	17%
8		Company D	18%
9		Company E	15%
10		Other	17%
11		Total	100%
13		Company	2015
14		Company A	20%
15		Company Aa	13%
16		Company B	0%
17		Company C	17%
18		Company D	18%
19		Company E	0%
20		Company F	5%
21		Company G	10%
22		Other	17%
23		Total	100%

11.3.3 BAR CHART

Individual object comparisons are represented using bar charts. The values are arranged along the straight axis, and the groups are grouped along the vertical axis in the Bar Chart. When one chooses to compare values through a few categories, organize the details in columns/rows on the spreadsheet to construct a Bar Chart. The figures are arranged horizontally.

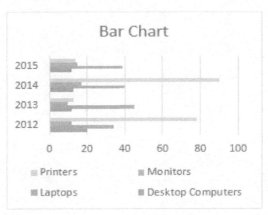

There are some different types of bar charts.

- **Horizontal Bar Charts** show data in a horizontal format. The data types are displayed on the vertical axis, while the data values are displayed on the horizontal axis.
- **Vertical Bar Charts** are also known as column charts. The numerical values expressed in the vertical bars are displayed by it. This is primarily used to display age and wage levels.
- **Grouped Bar Charts,** is a mix of various time span numbers that both belong to the same grouping.
- **Stacked Bar Charts** are a type of bar chart that depicts contrasts between data categories while still allowing for comparison and breakdown.
- **A Column Chart** shows groups on the horizontal side and the values on the vertical axes. Organize the information in columns or rows on the spreadsheet to make a column chart when one wants to evaluate values in a few different categories. The values are arranged vertically.

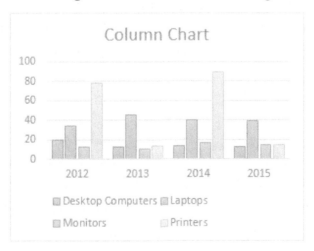

On an equally scaled axis, line charts will display continuous data over time. As a result, they're perfect for displaying data patterns at regular intervals, such as weeks, quarters, or decades. When one wants to see patterns over a long span of time, such as months, days, years, and so on.

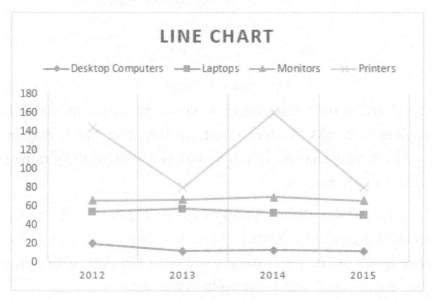

11.3.5 COMBO CHART

This chart combines 2 or more chart styles to make data easier to interpret, particularly when the data is complex. It has a secondary axis that makes it much simpler to learn. Organize the details in columns and rows on the spreadsheet to make a Combo table. When one wishes to draw attention to various categories of data.

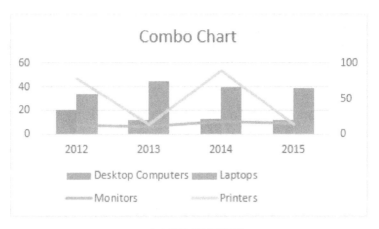

11.3.6 STOCK CHART

This chart, as the name suggests, will demonstrate market differences in stocks. A Stock chart, on the other hand, may be used to display changes in other statistics, such as daily rain or average temperatures.

Organize the details in columns/rows in a certain order on the spreadsheet to make a stock chart. To make a basic high-low-close Stock chart, for instance, organize the data with High, Low, & Close as Column names in that order.

11.3.7 BUBBLES CHART

This chart is similar to a Scatter chart, but it has a 3rd column that specifies the scale of the bubbles that display the data points in the data set.

11.3.8 AREA CHART

These charts are useful for plotting progress over time and highlighting the cumulative value across the trend. An area chart displays the association between sections to a whole by displaying the number of the plotted values. Organize the details in columns/rows on the spreadsheet to make an Area Chart.

When one needs to find the best combo of two sets of information, a Surface map comes in handy. Colors and shapes, much as on a topographic chart, denote regions with similar values.

11.3.10 IMPORTANCE OF CHARTS

- Charts let you visualize data graphically.

- It's better to evaluate trends, patterns in the charts.

- As opposed to data in cells, it's simple to understand.

- Data can be visualized (makes larger data easier to understand)

- Identify and categorize data.

- Find the relationship within the information.

- Know the concept of data.

- Recognize the data distribution.

- Realize the duplication of the data.

- Determine the patterns and developments.

- Identify outliers and other irregularities in the information.

- Anticipate upcoming developments.

- Tell interesting and entertaining tales to decision-makers.

Graphs depict changes in the values of data over a period of time. Since one is working with various data parameters, it is less complicated than charts. It's more complex to compare and contrast segments from the same information against one another.

If one wants to see how the number of hours working each week and the duration of annual leaves for the staff has changed over the last five years, they can make a clear line graph and watch the rises and dips and get a good idea.

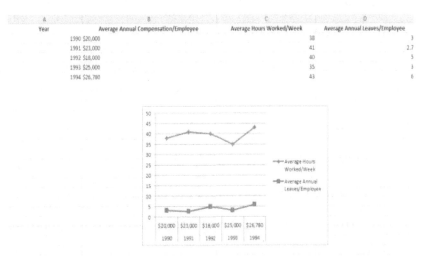

11.5 TYPES OF GRAPHS IN EXCEL

There are 3 types of graphs used in Excel:

11.5.1 LINE GRAPHS

In all versions of Microsoft Excel, all 2 dimensional and 3-dimensional line graphs are present. Line graphs are excellent for displaying long-term patterns. Plot several data parameters against one X-axis or period, such as job salary, the average amount of hours working/ week, and avg number of annual leaves.

11.5.2 COLUMN GRAPHS

Observers may also use column graphs to see if parameters shift over time. If only one data parameter is included, they are referred to as "graphs." When several parameters are active, users are unable to gain much input into how every parameter has improved. When the avg. no. of hours worked /week and the avg. no of annual leaves are plotted side by side, as seen in the Column graph below, the avg. no. of hours worked/ week and the avg. no. of annual leaves do not have the same consistency as the Line graph.

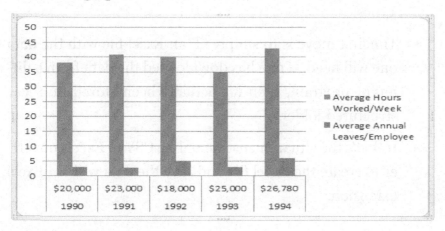

These are identical to column graphs in that the constant variable is allocated to Y-axis, and the parameters are measured against the X-axis.

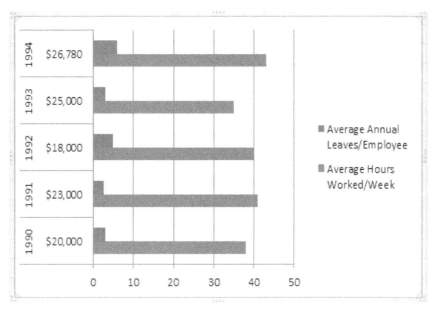

11.6 CREATING GRAPHS & CHARTS IN EXCEL

- Add the data to the Excel Sheet & Allocate the Right Data Types.

- The first move is to simply fill an Excel file with the data one will need. If one has downloaded the data from a different program, then it's actually been stored in a .csv structured folder.

- If that's the situation, use an online CSV to Excel converter to create the Excel file and save the data with an Excel extension.

- After transforming the file, one will need to tidy up the rows and columns. It is easier to start on a clean worksheet so that the Excel graph one is making is clean and simple to edit or update.

- Excel has two elements of the spreadsheets:

- Rows are horizontal and labeled with numbers.

- Columns are vertical and labeled with alphabets.

- Once all the information values have been set and checked for, ensure that one visits the Number section underneath the Home tab and adds the correct data form to the different columns. If one does not do this, the odds are the graphs may not come up correctly.

- If column B is calculating time, for instance, make sure one chooses Time from the drop-down menu and allocates it to B.

- Choose the kind of graph one wants to make based on the details they have and the number of different criteria they will be monitoring at the same time.

- Line graphs are the best choice if one wants to keep track of patterns over time.

- Assume one is looking at the Avg Number of Hours Worked and Avg Number of Leaves, Employees, or years for a 5 period.

- Select the data sets one would like to analyze.

- One must choose the various data parameters in order to build a graph.

- Bring the pointer over the cell labeled A to do so. It will change into a small arrow pointing down. When this occurs, simply click on cell A to pick the whole column, repeat the operation same with columns B and C.

Click the Ctrl button on Windows or the Command key on Mac.

This is what the final collection could look like:

	A	B	C
C1		fx Average Number of Leaves/Employee/Year	
1	Year	Average Hours Worked/Week/Employee	Average Number of Leaves/Employee/Year
2	01-01-1990	38.00	3.00
3	01-01-1991	41.00	2.70
4	01-01-1992	40.00	5.00
5	01-01-1993	35.00	3.00
6	01-01-1994	43.00	6.00
7			

As the columns are chosen, go to the Insert tab and select 2D Line Graph from the drop-down menu.

A graph will show below the data values right away.

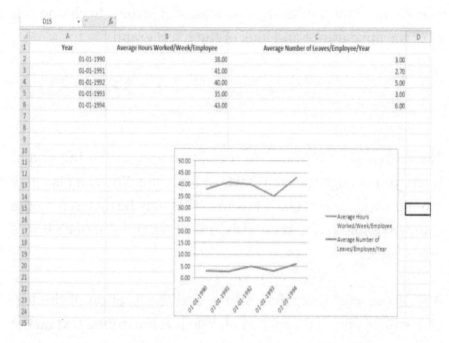

If one does not allocate the correct data from the columns during the first stage, the graph may not display the way you like. Rather than the Year, Excel might graph the parameter of Avg. Number of Leaves, Employee, or Year along the X-axis. In this scenario, one can use the Switch Row and Column choice under the Chart Tools Design tab to experiment with the different X-axis and Y-axis parameter combinations before one finds the right representation.

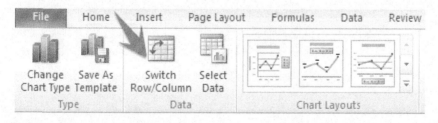

Go over to Chart Tools in the header to adjust the colors or design of the graph.

You have a choice of design, format, and layout. Each one can alter the appearance and look of the Excel graph.

The design key helps one to reposition and switch the graph. It lets you change the chart style at any time. You can also play around with various chart layouts. This may be dictated by the company's marketing standards, one's own style, or one's boss's preferences.

11.6.1 LAYOUT

Adjust the axis' title, chart's title, and the location of the legend with layouts. Vertical text on Y-axis & horizontal text on the X-axis are two options. The grid lines can also be changed. To change the look and design of the graph, one has access to any formatting method imaginable.

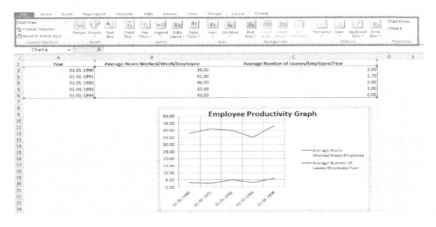

This tab helps one to introduce a border across the graph of choice in width and color, separating it from the data points that occupy the rows & columns.

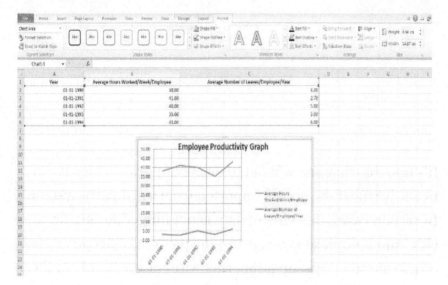

One can conveniently construct a graph while working with basic data sets.

However, there would be bugs if one starts putting in several forms of data with various variables. The below are some of the obstacles one will face:

When making graphs, data sorting may be a challenge. Data sorting can be recommended in online tutorials to make the "charts" more visually appealing. As the X-axis is a time-based parameter. Since the dates are ordered randomly, sorting data **values by magnitude can disrupt the graph's flow. It's possible** that one won't be able to identify the patterns very well.

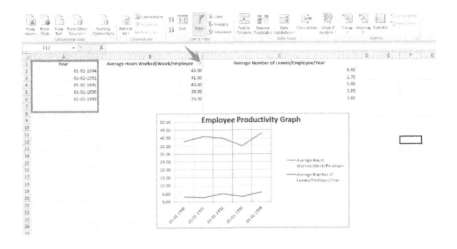

It's possible that one will fail to delete duplicates. This is particularly true if the data is imported from a 3rd party system. In certain cases, this kind of data is not filtered for inefficiencies. And if duplicates creep into the pictorial reflection of patterns, one could end up tampering with the credibility of the data. When dealing with large amounts of info, the Remove Duplicates feature on the rows is the right approach.

Constructing graphs in Excel doesn't have to be difficult, but there are several simpler options available.

11.7 CREATING CHARTS WITH MS EXCEL

Take these measures to make a chart:

- Decide which data to use in the graph. Include all cells with text marks that can be used in the chart as well.

For this step, one may need to use a set of cells that aren't adjacent to each other (noncontiguous). If this is the case, keep the Ctrl key pressed when selecting the cells one wants.

- Choose a chart from the Insert tab. (Use the Charts group's buttons.)

The chart subtypes will be shown on the menu.

11.7.1 SELECT THE DESIRED SUBTYPE BY CLICKING ON IT

- A chart will be produced and put as a floating image on the current spreadsheet.
- One can resize the chart. Push or pull one of the frame's corners or one of the side's pick sticks (shown by many dots).

- One can move the chart. Except for the corner or a side collection handle, drag any portion of the chart.
- One can place it on the new tab. Select Design, then Move Chart from the drop-down menu. Then press New Sheet in the Move Chart dialogue box, then ok.

If the data in the chart isn't what one thought it would be, try 1 of the following techniques:

- Remove the map and try again for various ranges this time.
- Choose Design, then go to Data, then Switch Row/Column to change the way the data is represented.
- Choose Design, then go to Data, then Select Data to change which cells are included in the table.

11.7.2 CHANGE THE CHART'S STYLE

At any moment, one can quickly move to a different chart style.

Select your chart.

In the Type group of the Design tab, press Change Chart Type.

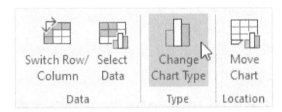

Select column from the left side.

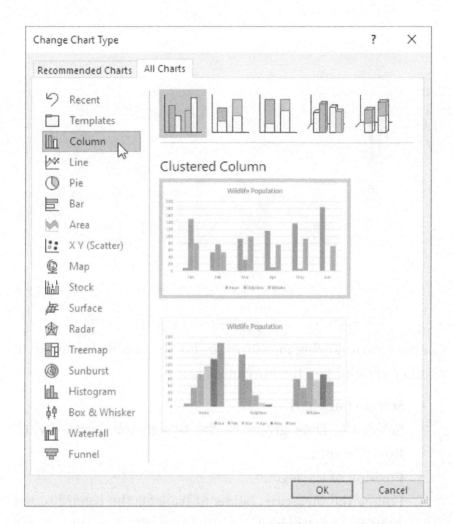

Once you have made the decision, press ok.

This will be the result.

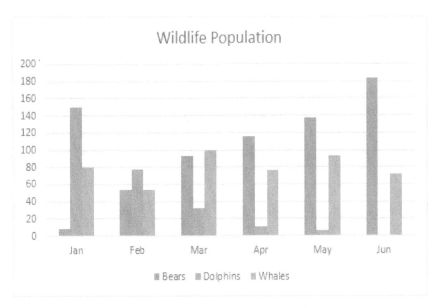

11.7.3 ROW/COLUMN SWITCHING

Conduct the following measures to show a variable (rather than another variable) on the horizontal axis.

- Select your chart.
- Select the Data group in the Design tab, press Switch Row/Column.
- Position of the legend.
- Follow the measures below to transfer the legend to the right side of the chart.
- Select your chart.
- On the right side of the chart, press the + button, then the arrow next to Legend, then Right.

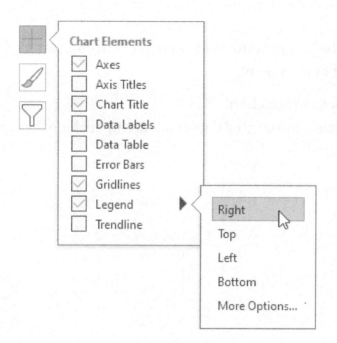

As a result,

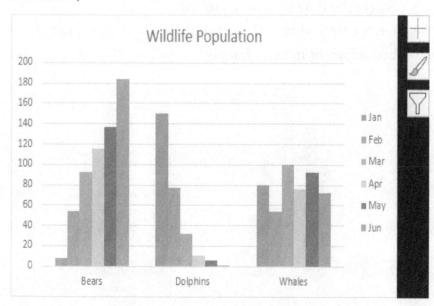

171

Data labels may be used to draw readers' interest in a certain data set or data point.

- Select your chart.
- Select the wanted data sequence by clicking the green bar.

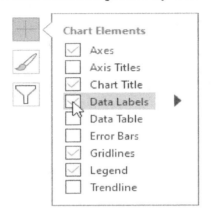

- Select the data one wants to use.
- On the right side of the chart, press the + icon and tick the box adjacent to Data Labels.

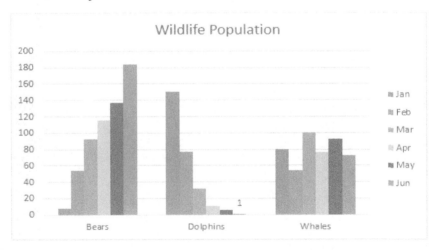

172

One may also create the table in Excel using currently existing data, so they don't need to create data visualization. A data collection may be formatted as a table in 2 ways:

The first way is to do it manually. One can manually insert data and format it as a table by adding column & row names in this case.

The second way is to use Excel's Format as Table Preset function to enter raw data (with no column and row names).

To display data as the table, click and move the pointer over the cells that contain the data set, then choose the Home tab and then select Format as Table from the drop-down menu on the toolbar.

Format
as Table

Choose New Table Style... from the drop-down menu. (One will also see a PivotTables option.)

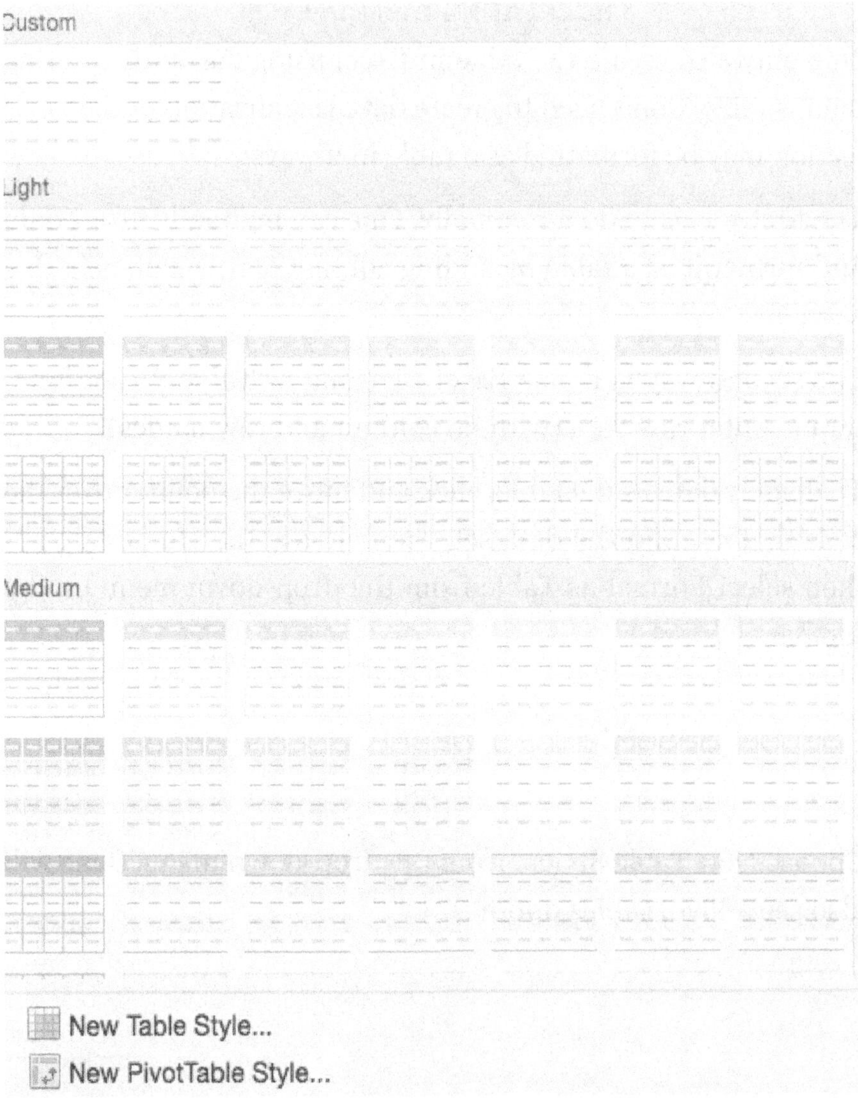

Custom

Light

Medium

New Table Style...

New PivotTable Style...

A dialogue box appears, allowing one to specify which elements of the chosen set should be included in the formatted table. To continue, press the blue OK icon.

BOOK 12
Benefits & Applications of Microsoft Excel

12.1 APPLICATIONS OF MICROSOFT EXCEL

12.1.1 DATA ANALYSIS AND STORAGE

Among the most useful features of Excel is the ability to review vast volumes of data in order to spot patterns. One could summarize data and organize it in an orderly manner with the assistance of charts and graphs so that one can quickly access it anytime they need it. It becomes simpler to store records, and one can save a lot of time as a result.

Data may be utilized for a variety of applications once it has been stored in a structured manner. Microsoft Excel makes it easy to perform different operations on data by including a variety of resources.

12.1.2 EXCEL'S APPLICATIONS HELP ONE TO DO THE JOB FASTER AND MORE EFFI-CIENTLY

Microsoft Excel has a plethora of resources that make the job a lot easier and saves one time. There are incredible resources for browsing, sorting, and scanning that make the job much easier.

One will complete the job in even less time if they mix these methods with tables, pivot tables, and other tools. Multiple components can be conveniently included in vast volumes of data to assist in the solution of a variety of issues and queries.

12.1.3 SPREADSHEETS & DATA RECOVERY

Another advantageous feature of Microsoft Excel makes it is easier, in case if the data is damaged, one will easily regain it. If an entrepreneur has valuable data saved in Excel and it is missing, or the file is destroyed, they need not fear since the Excel XML format will be used to recover the lost or broken file data.

The next significant application is that MS Excel worksheets make the task easier, and it can shrink the size of the spreadsheet and make things lightweight quickly with the current Excel XML format.

12.1.4 MS EXCEL'S MATHEMATICAL CALCULATIONS MAKE THE CALCULATION SIMPLER

The very good use of Excel is that it allows one to solve complicated mathematical problems in a far easier and less time-consuming manner.

There are several formulas in Excel, and by using them, one will perform a variety of operations on a vast volume of data at once, such as finding the count, average, and so on.

As a result, Microsoft Excel is used anytime people need to solve complicated mathematical problems or add basic mathematical formulas to tables with a lot of details.

12.1.5 SECURITY

The most important feature of Microsoft Excel is that it secures Excel archives, allowing users to keep their data protected. Via simple visual coding or directly inside the excel file, all Excel files may be passcode protected.

Companies keep their valuable data in MS Excel so they can keep it sorted and save time. Mostly everyone needs their data to be password locked so that no one may access them or destroy them, and MS Excel is an excellent solution to this issue.

12.1.6 GET DATA DISPLAYS MORE SOPHISTICATEDLY

The next benefit of MS Excel is that it allows one to bring more functionality to the data presentations, which ensures one can refine the data bars, highlight any relevant things they wish to highlight, and quickly make the data more visually appealing.

If one has data stored in Microsoft Excel and wishes to illustrate something significant, they can use the different data presentation features included in the Excel. One might also make the spreadsheets on which they have processed data more appealing.

Another advantage of Excel is that it can be downloaded online from everywhere at any time, allowing one to use it from any platform and from every place. It allows us to function more efficiently, which ensures even if one does not have a computer, they can use someone else phone to complete their tasks quickly and effectively. As a result of the extensive versatility that Microsoft Excel offers, people want to work on it so that anyone can focus on their work without being distracted by their smartphone or venue.

12.1.8 KEEPS ALL OF THE DATA IN ONE PLACE

Another useful feature of Microsoft Excel is that it allows one to have all of their data in one place. It will assist them in preventing the loss of their records. It will keep all of their data in one place, so they won't have to spend time looking for files. As a result, one can spend less time and will be able to quickly look up the organized and sorted data anytime they need it.

12.1.9 ASSISTS BUSINESSPEOPLE IN IMPLEMENTING LONG-TERM STRATEGIES

Data may be represented in the form of graphs and charts to aid in the identification of various patterns. Trend lines may be expanded far beyond the graph with the support of Microsoft Excel, making it far simpler to analyze insights and changes.

In order to increase profits, it is crucial to analyze the appeal of products or the selling trend that they adopt. Excel makes this challenge easier for company owners, allowing them to flourish and increase earnings.

12.1.10 MANAGE EXPENSES

Microsoft Excel is useful for budgeting. For example, if a specialist earns $50,000 each month, he would pay certain costs, and if he needs to know precisely how much he spends each month, he will quickly do so with Excel. He will enter his monthly revenue and expenditures into excel tables to see how much he is investing, allowing him to manage his finances further.

MS Excel has many advantages; that's why users use it all around the globe for a variety of activities. Not only can it save resources, but it also helps the job simpler. It is almost capable of doing any mission. For e.g., one can perform quantitative calculations as well as create graphical representations to store data. It is easy for a businessperson to quantify and store data in it.

12.2 BUSINESS USES FOR MICROSOFT EXCEL

12.2.1 MS EXCEL HAS THE ABILITY TO STORE AND INTERPRET VAST AMOUNTS OF DATA

It helps to maintain all of the details in one location so that it does not get misplaced and time is not wasted looking for specific information.

It has become such a common program as a result of these reasons, and people have become accustomed to using it. Entry and preservation of data.

Excel is a great platform for data entry and storing at the simplest stage. The only restriction to the size of an Excel file is the processing capacity and memory of the computer. At best, 1,048,576 rows & 16,384 columns can be placed on a spreadsheet. Excel will clearly hold a lot of information. Not only that, but features like Data Form make it simple to enter and display data, allowing consumers to build personalized data entry forms adapted to their unique business requirements. Which will be used to create and manage client mailing lists as well as staff change rosters.

12.2.2 BUSINESS DATA COLLECTION & VERIFICATION

Businesses often use different structures (such as CRM and inventory) within each database log. All of this information can be translated to Excel for quick entry. The software may also be used to tidy up data by deleting redundant or missing entries; removing those data from the start is critical since it can affect subsequent review and reporting.

12.2.3 ADMINISTRATIVE & MANAGEMENT RESPONSIBILITIES

Developing and outlining business procedures is one part of management responsibilities.

This helps in the optimization of processes and is a useful method for planning operations and situations. Excel has software for creating flow charts with text, images, and illustrations.

12.2.4 BUDGETING & ACCOUNTING

Excel also comes with accounting and budgeting models that are easy to use. The software's integrated measuring and formula tools will then be used to help one coordinate and summarize the findings.

12.2.5 EXAMINE THE DATA

So one has been given a mountain of data and the task of extracting information from it. Excel will also help them handle and formulate simple, communicable data, so don't stress. Pivot Tables are one of the main qualities for this. They enable users to condense and concentrate on specific data segments from a broad data collection, resulting in brief observations that can be used as an immersive overview report. The table may be easily modified to represent preferred data fields by adding filters or switching out data columns.

12.2.6 VISUALIZATIONS AND REPORTING

Graphs, charts can be created using data from both direct data sets and Pivot tables and may be used in written papers, interviews, or as a data collection tool. Since they may give a different viewpoint on patterns and results. Excel has a number of pre-made map models, but it also enables consumers to customize shades, axis values, and text remarks. Visual reporting may be applied to every industry. A column table, for example, may be used by marketing departments to check on the effectiveness of an advertising campaign over time and to equate it to past initiatives.

12.2.7 ASSUMPTION

Although monitoring and updating performance is critical in every sector, planning and preparing for different scenarios and adjustments is equally crucial. When designed to simulate financial forecasts using historical evidence, Excel may be used in combination with third-party applications. Excel may also generate a function from the data collection of a map that can be used to determine potential values.

12.3 BENEFITS OF USING MS EXCEL

12.3.1 ACCOUNTING

Budgeting, forecasting, expense monitoring, financial reporting, loan spreadsheets, and more are all available on Excel.

This software was essentially created to satisfy these various accounting requirements. Excel clearly suits the bill since it is used by 89 percent of businesses for multiple accounting functions.

Excel also comes with a variety of spreadsheet models to help you with all of these tasks.

12.3.2 GRAPHING

The list continues on and on with pie charts, line charts, bar charts, scatter charts, area charts, and column charts. Excel's ability to turn rows and columns of numbers into stunning charts is sure to become one of the favorite features if one needs to reflect data more interactive and easy to digest.

12.3.3 INVENTORY MANAGEMENT

It may be difficult to keep track of the inventory. Luckily, Excel may assist employees, company owners, and even people in keeping track of their products, so no big issues arise.

12.3.4 SCHEDULES & CALENDARS

If one needs to plan their blog or website's material calendar? Is one looking for lesson plans for their classroom? Is there a paid vacation schedule for one and their coworkers? A regular routine for one's family? When it comes to different schedules, Excel can be a fairly good option.

12.3.5 SEATING TABLES

Creating a seating chart for anything from a major corporate feast to a wedding can be a royal pain. Thankfully, Excel will render it an absolute breeze. If one is a total whiz, they will be able to build the seating chart using their spreadsheet of RSVPs instantly. Excel will provide assistance yon in completing all tasks.

12.3.6 WORKSHEET FOR GOAL SETTING

It benefits from having anything to hold yourself centered as well as on the track, whether it's career aspirations, health goals, or financial goals. Excel's charm is identified. One will use the software to build a variety of worksheets, logs, and preparation papers to track their success and, ideally, reach the finish line.

12.3.7 MOCK-UPS

When that it comes to programming, Excel may not be the first thing that comes to mind. However, accept it or not, the platform may be used to create different mock-ups and designs. It's a common option for designing website prototypes and workflows, in reality.

12.3.8 COMPLETE YOUR TASKS

If one wants to increase their productivity. On the other hand, Excel will come to the rescue with a multitude of functions that can help one manage their activities and to-dos with simplicity and organization.

12.3.9 TASK LIST

Say farewell to the old-fashioned to-do list on paper. With Excel, you can create a much more comprehensive task list and chart the progress on the bigger tasks one already has on one plate.

12.3.10 ITEM LISTS

Similarly, one should make a quick checklist to cross off the items they have bought or completed—from a shopping list to a list of to-dos for a forthcoming publicity campaign.

12.3.11 SCHEMATICS FOR PROJECT MANAGEMENT

Excel is a complete package when it comes to making charts. This principle is often applicable when it comes to different project management maps.

Excel will help maintain their project on track in a variety of ways, from waterfall maps to many styles of charts to monitor the team's success.

12.3.12 TIMESHEETS

You also realize that keeping track of the time will help you be more productive. Although there are several fancy applications and software to help you fulfill the need, think of Excel as the initial time-tracking application. It continues to be a viable alternative today.

12.3.13 TYPES OF DOCUMENTS

Excel is a wonderful tool for constructing shapes, from basic to complex. One can even program numerous dropdown tariffs so that consumers can choose from a pre-defined list of options.

12.3.14 QUIZZES

It is a good way to find your knowledge of a certain subject, anyone else, or your students in Excel. One will build a set of queries in one spreadsheet and then order Excel to quiz you or another person.

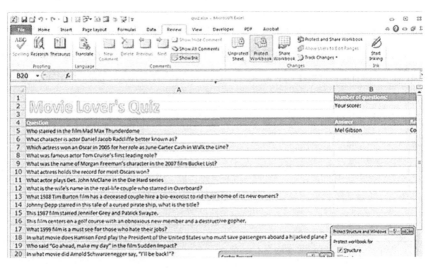

Managing partnerships is vital to progress both professionally and socially. Surprisingly, Excel makes it easier to stay in contact.

12.3.16 CRM

CRM Template
[Your Name]

Name	Company	Work Function	Phone	Email	Estimated Sale	Last Contact	Next Action	Next Contact	Lead Status	Lead Source	Notes
Jameson, Bill	XYZ Plumbing	Owner	444-555-6666	xyz@plumber.com	$ 45,000	1/10/13		1/29/13	Cold	Referral	
Anderson, Jane	ABC Corp	Sales Manager	222-656-7890	busi@abccorp.com	$ 10,000	1/25/13		2/5/13	Warm	Website	
Smithers, Joe	ACME	Business Dev.	111-234-5678	acme@acme.com	$ 4,500	1/27/13		2/15/13	Active	Email	Loves chocolate

Insert new rows above the gray line

Need a compact CRM to keep top of mind with the customers? One should build one in Excel. And the greatest news? Creating your own ensures it would be completely customizable. Sales Programmer has put together a handy series of free sales excel models one can use to help them get started.

12.3.17 E-MAIL LIST

	A	B	C	D	E	F
1	FIRST NAME	LAST NAME	ADDRESS	CITY	STATE	ZIP CODE
2	Oprah	Winfrey	123 Magnificent Mile Ave.	Chicago	IL	58922
3	Mister	Rodgers	8935 Beautiful Day Rd.	New York	NY	23935
4	Hulk	Hogan	9284 Hollywood Blvd.	Los Angeles	CA	39825

Data does not often have to be numerical, Or Excel is also excellent at handling and sorting huge lists of addresses and phone numbers, making it ideal for the business's holiday party invitation list or the mailing list for a vast promotion, project, or campaign.

One may also mail, combine using Excel, which allows printing shipping labels and other resources a lot simpler. A similar definition may also be used to build folders, RSVP lists, and other lists that provide a lot of knowledge about individuals.

12.3.18 IT'S ALL FOR ENTERTAINMENT

It doesn't have to be all job and no play when it comes to Excel. One may make a variety of other interesting items with the spreadsheet tool.

12.3.19 LOGBOOKS FROM THE PAST

If one wants to keep track of the different draught drinks they have tried, the exercises one has done, or anything else, Excel will help them keep it organized and recorded.

Workout Log

Stats

Average Duration (minutes)	Average Calories
35	402
Average Distance (miles/km)	Average Weight
2.75	131
Average Pace (per hour)	
4.88	

Workouts

DATE	ACTIVITY	DURATION (minutes)	DISTANCE (miles/km)	PACE (per hour)	CALORIES	WEIGHT	NOTES
6/18/17	Cross Trainer	40	2.50	3.75	380	132	[Notes]
8/20/17	Treadmill	30	3.00	6.00	423	130	[Notes]

12.3.20 SUDOKU

Sudoku is a form of crossword puzzle. Do you like Sudoku puzzles? One should make their own in Excel, as it turns out. Alternatively, if one is stuck on an especially difficult one, they should recruit the assistance of Excel to help them work it out.

12.3.21 WORDS CLOUDS

These aren't the most scientific way to view results. They are, though, an enjoyable (not to mention gorgeous) way to learn about the most commonly used phrases. You guessed it—Excel can be used to create one. MS Excel is commonly used for a variety of uses because data is easily saved, and material can be inserted and deleted with no effort.

The below are some of the most significant advantages of using Microsoft Excel:

12.3.22 DATA STORAGE

MS Excel is commonly used to store and analyze data because there is no limitation to the volume of data that may be stored in a worksheet.

- Filtering data in Excel is simple and straightforward.
- Easy to Restore Files: Locating data written on paper can take longer, but that isn't the case for Excel worksheets.
- It's simple to locate and recover files.
- Use of Mathematical Calculations: Using the formulas method in Microsoft Excel, doing calculations has been simpler and less time-consuming.
- More Security: As compared to data written in records or on a sheet of paper. They are not protected, these spreadsheets may be password protected on a desktop or personal device, and the risk of missing them is much lower.
-

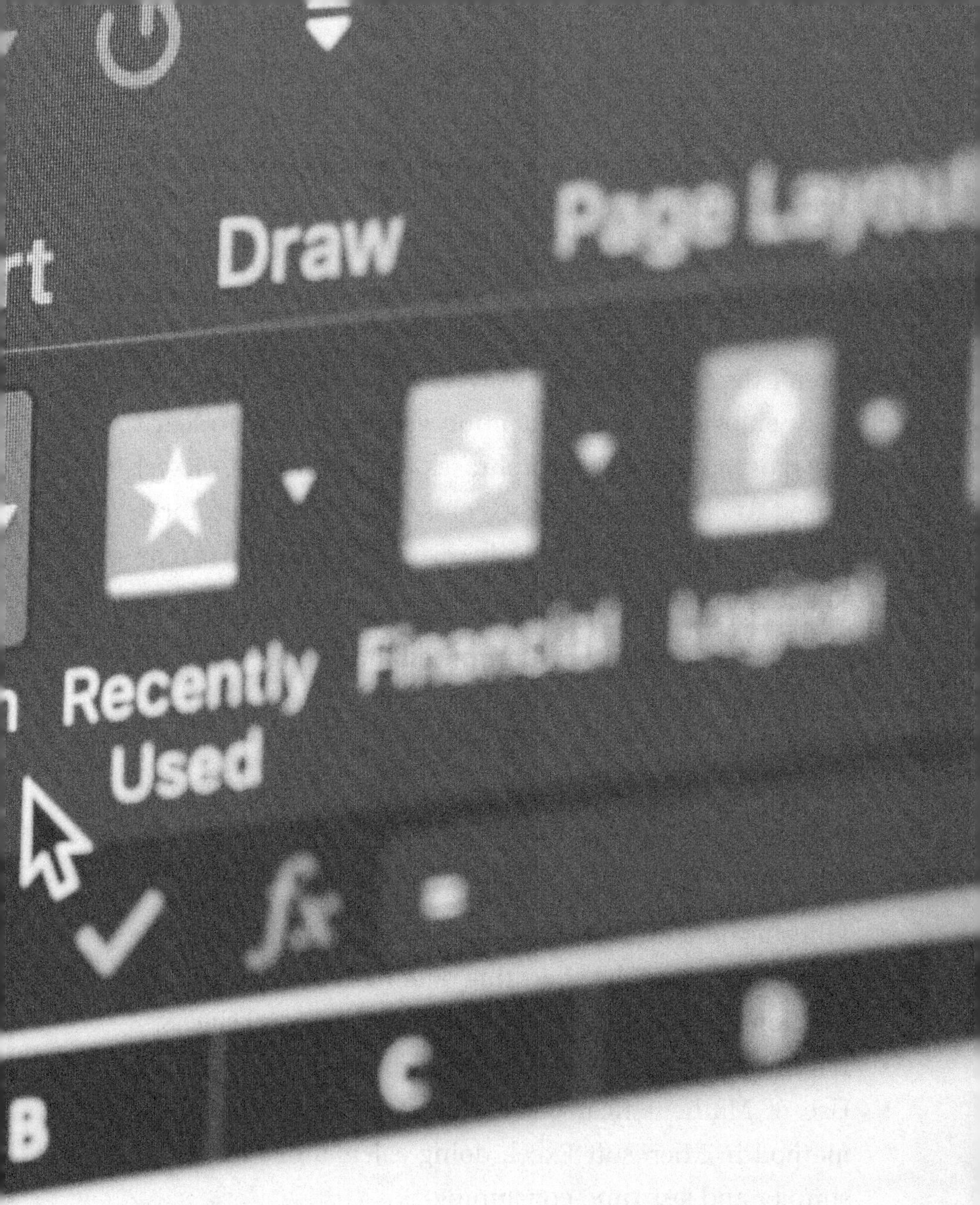

Recently
Used

Financial

Layout

B

100+
VIDEO TUTORIALS ARE HERE:

https://youtube.com/playlist?list=PLWPirh4EWFpEp
O6NjjWLbKSCb-wx3hMql&si=Tug8oaQf2K50FPD3

BOOK 13
Tips, Shortcuts & Techniques
for Microsoft Excel

13.1 WHY USE EXCEL SHORTCUTS?

Using shortcuts in excel or shortcut keys is a somewhat overlooked way of efficiency while operating with an Excel model. When using shortcuts rather than clicking in the toolbar, these shortcut keys execute big functions that greatly improve performance and speed. Consider hitting just 2-3 keys on the keyboard rather than shifting the hand to the cursor, moving the button, then clicking several times.

There are hundreds of keyboard Excel shortcuts available to help one get something done in Excel. These shortcuts may be used for a variety of tasks, ranging from basic worksheet navigation to formula filling and data sorting.

13.1.1 EXCEL BASICS' SHORTCUTS

Before moving into Excel shortcuts, it's a good idea to go through the common vocabulary for the various Excel components.

- Any of the several boxes in the Excel worksheet is referred to as a cell.

- The active cell is the one that Excel is actually selecting. There could only be 1 functioning cell at any given time.

- The active cell, or a community of cells, is referred to as a selection. If the range contains more than 1 cell, the active cell will be outlined in white, whereas the remainder of the selection will be grey.

- A column is a collection of vertical cells in Excel referred to by letters ranging from A-Z. Excel can duplicate letters the second time after column Z. As a result, and column AA is the next column after column Z, preceded by column AB.

- A row is a set of horizontal cells in Excel that are referred to by integers in ascending order from 1-n. The value of n varies depending on the version and Excel edition.

Inside Excel, there are many various types of data.

- Text is a type of data that is made up of letters. Text data may also contain numbers. On the other hand, these quantities must be used in combination with letters or specific to the text.

- Numbers are records that are solely made up of numbers. Digit-type data could not use characters, unlike text-type data, which does.

- Numbers are used in combination with a currency marker in currency and accounting information.

- Dates are bits of information that represent a date and/or period. In Excel, dates may be formatted in a variety of ways.

- Data of the percentage kind is a form of numbered data that has been translated to a %. These can be translated back into data of the number kind, and likewise. When one converts a % to an integer, the result is a decimal. 89 percent, for example, would be converted to 0.89.

13.2 SHORTCUTS FOR THE MICROSOFT EXCEL

Here are some shortcuts for your ease. For people using windows, use the ctrl key and for Mac users, use the command key.

- Shift+F1 is for Opening the "What's This?" frame.

- Ctrl+F3 is for Opening Excel Name Manager.

- Shift+F3 is for Opening the Excel formula window.

- Alt+Shift+F2 is for saving the recent spreadsheet.
- Shift+F5 is for Bringing up the search box.
- Shift+F6 is for Moving to the previous lane.
- Shift+F9 is for performing calculating functions on the recent sheet.
- Ctrl+F5 is for restoring window size.
- Shift+F8 is for Adding to selection.
- Shift+F2 is for allowing a person to edit the cell comment.
- Ctrl+F6 is for opening the Next workbook.
- Ctrl+Shift+F6 is for the previous workbook.
- Ctrl+F7 is for moving the window.
- Alt+F2 is for saving as an option.
- Ctrl+Shift+F3 is for creating names using either columns or row labels.
- Ctrl+F8 is for resizing the window.
- Ctrl+F9 is for minimizing the current window.
- Ctrl+Shift+F6 is for Moving to the previous spreadsheet window.
- Ctrl+F4 is for the Closing recent window.
- Ctrl+F10 is for maximizing the presently selected window.
- Ctrl+F11 is for inserting a macro sheet.
- Ctrl+F12 is for Opening a file.
- Ctrl+Shift+F12 is for printing the present spreadsheet.

- Alt+F1 is for inserting a chart.

- Alt+Shift+F1 the macro Creating the new spreadsheet.

- Alt+F4 is for Exiting Excel.

- Alt+F8 is for the Opening dialog box for the macro.

- Alt+F11 is the macro Opening Visual Basic editor.

File

Create new workbook	Ctrl N	⌘ N
Open workbook	Ctrl O	⌘ O
Save workbook	Ctrl S	⌘ S
Save as	F12	⌘ ⇧ S
Print file	Ctrl P	⌘ P
Open print preview window	Ctrl F2	
Close current workbook	Ctrl W	⌘ W
Close Excel	Alt F4	⌘ Q
Open options	Alt F T	⌘ ,
Open help	F1	⌘ /
Undo last action	Ctrl Z	⌘ Z
Redo last action	Ctrl Y	⌘ Y
Copy selected cells	Ctrl C	⌘ C
Repeat last action	F4	⌘ Y
Cut selected cells	Ctrl X	⌘ X
Paste content from clipboard	Ctrl V	⌘ V
Display the Paste Special dialog box	Ctrl Alt V	⌘ ^ V
Display find and replace	Ctrl F	⌘ F
Display find and replace, replace selected	Ctrl H	^ H
Find previous match	Ctrl Shift F4	⌘ ⇧ G

	Windows	Mac
Insert table	Ctrl T	^ T
Toggle Autofilter	Ctrl Shift L	⌘ ⇧ F
Activate filter	Alt ↓	⌥ ↓
Select table row	Shift Space	⇧ Space
Select table column	Ctrl Space	^ Space
Select table	Ctrl A	⌘ A
Clear slicer filter	Alt C	⌥ C
Toggle table total row	Ctrl Shift T	⌘ ⇧ T

13.3 KEYBOARD SHORTCUTS

If you've mastered the keyboard shortcuts, you'll save a lot of time and be able to maneuver like an expert. Here are a few favorites:

- Ctrl + A is for will selecting all of the data.

- Shift + Space is for selecting rows of their active cell.

- Ctrl + C is for copying the selected data.

- Ctrl + Down Arrow is for taking the user to the last cell of their active column.

- Ctrl + V is for pasting the copied data.

- Shift + Space is for selecting rows of their active cell.

- Ctrl + End is for taking the user to the last cell of their data.

- Ctrl + minus sign is for giving the user Delete options.

- **Ctrl + Up Arrow is for taking the user to the first cell of their active column.**

- Ctrl + Space is for selecting a column of their active cell.

- Ctrl + Home is for taking the user to the first cell of their data.

13.4 TIPS & TECHNIQUES

13.4.1 MATCHING INDEXES

It is one of the most effective Excel role combos. It can be used to find a value in a large table of information and return a value within that table. Let's assume the one organization has 900 people, and they have a worksheet with all of their records, including salaries, start date, direct supervisor, and so on. However, one supervisor has a staff of 20 people, and they are just focused on them. INDEX-MATCH can search the table for the information of those specific team members (which must be special, such as an email address or an employee identity no.) and display the desired details for the team. It's worth the time to get your mind around this because it's more versatile and efficient than VLOOKUPs.

13.4.2 INCREASE THE NUMBER OF LEADING ZEROES

One may need to add leading zeroes to the series if the value obtained is almost always in text format.

For e.g., one would want to display the no. 8192 as 0000008192, converting it to a ten-character text meaning. If one has a no. in A1 that they want to translate to text with leading zeroes, enter such formula in B1 and a maxi. Length of ten characters.

`=TEXT(A1,REPT("0",10))`

	A	B	C
54	Number	Formatted	Formula
55	589	000000589	=TEXT(A55,REPT("0",9))
56	55555	000055555	=TEXT(A56,REPT("0",9))
57	999999999	999999999	=TEXT(A57,REPT("0",9))

13.4.3 REPEAT HEADER FOR PRINTING

It's helpful to replicate the header row(s) on each page when printing a many-page cover. To do the same, go to the ribbon's Page Layout menu choice.

Choose the Print Titles choice. In the Rows to Replicate at Top box, choose the row or rows one wishes to repeat at the top.

13.4.4 NAME THE RANGES

For spreadsheets with a wide number of rows, giving ranges names makes it easier to refer to them in formulas without having to press and pick long ranges. To easily name the ranges, use the following formula:

- On the ribbon, choose the Formulas menu choice.

- Choose to Create from Selection on the dropdown menu.

- Normally, choose the ranges from which to assign names. Since the top row is the header row, it fits well.

13.4.5 FINDING A LINKED VALUE

Frequently, one must convert or cross-walk a value, such as a state code, to a similar value, such as the completely spelled state name. One can compose many embedded |IF| statements, but a |VLOOKUP| formula is a more export approach phrasing of the VLOOKUP formula is:

=VLOOKUP (lookup value then table array then column index numbs then range lookup). In the illustration above, the lookup value= state code, the table list is a table containing the state codes and definitions.

After matching the code, the column index is a column one wants to return to.

The range lookup statement allows one to look for precise (One or TRUE) or estimated results (Zero or FALSE)

Let's presume one has their consumer IDs in one Column, their mailing state code in another Column, and they want the state spelled out in the third Column. To do the same, take the following steps:

 In Columns 4th & 5th, make the table of codes and their full-spelled values.

Enter the following formula in the third column considering one column is A and 5th is F, and the rest comes in between. VLOOKUP = (B2, E3:F6,2,0)

Copy the formula down.

This is how it appears:

	A	B	C	D	E	F
1	ID	StateCode	StateDesc	Formula in column C		
2	395	OH	Ohio	=VLOOKUP(B2,$E$3:$F$6,2,0)	LookupValue	ReturnValue
3	156	MI	Michigan	=VLOOKUP(B3,$E$3:$F$6,2,0)	CA	California
4	460	VA	Virginia	=VLOOKUP(B4,$E$3:$F$6,2,0)	OH	Ohio
5	312	CA	California	=VLOOKUP(B5,$E$3:$F$6,2,0)	MI	Michigan
6	273	OH	Ohio	=VLOOKUP(B6,$E$3:$F$6,2,0)	VA	Virginia
7	393	CA	California	=VLOOKUP(B7,$E$3:$F$6,2,0)		
8	486	MI	Michigan	=VLOOKUP(B8,$E$3:$F$6,2,0)		
9						

Have you ever needed to transform the number column to distinct ranges to make summaries or graphs simpler? Have you ever wished there was an easier way to do something? There is, however: the |VLOOKUP| formula. You noticed the formula: =VLOOKUP (lookup value, table array, column index numb, range lookup) uses the |range lookup| statement with the value of |TRUE| to transform numbers to ranges, which tells Excel to create an estimated fit to the lookup value.

One should take advantage of this. Let's assume one has some data in Column A, such as population, earnings, prices, number of units, and so on. They would l You'd like to translate these values into specific ranges. To do so, take the following steps:

- In Columns F and G, make a table of steps and their distinct ranges.
- Enter the following formula in |C2|: =VLOOKUP (A2, F3:G8,2,1)

This is how it appears:

	A	B	C	D E	F	G
1	Measure	Range	Formula in column B			
2	48	0-49	=VLOOKUP(A2,$F$3:$G$8,2,1)		Measure	Ranges
3	701	500-999	=VLOOKUP(A3,$F$3:$G$8,2,1)		0	0-49
4	121	100-199	=VLOOKUP(A4,$F$3:$G$8,2,1)		50	50-99
5	527	500-999	=VLOOKUP(A5,$F$3:$G$8,2,1)		100	100-199
6	33	0-49	=VLOOKUP(A6,$F$3:$G$8,2,1)		200	200-499
7	483	200-499	=VLOOKUP(A7,$F$3:$G$8,2,1)		500	500-999
8	977	500-999	=VLOOKUP(A8,$F$3:$G$8,2,1)		1000	1000+
9	436	200-499	=VLOOKUP(A9,$F$3:$G$8,2,1)			
10	589	500-999	=VLOOKUP(A10,$F$3:$G$8,2,1)			
11	1001	1000+	=VLOOKUP(A11,$F$3:$G$8,2,1)			
12						

Have you ever seen a large amount of data in a text document and wished you could quickly copy it to Excel? Assume one has Word information with the following bullet points:

- Retailer A: 6,000 dollars.
- Retailer X: 8,900 dollars.
- Retailer D: 11,000 dollars.
- Retailer Z: 4,500 dollars.

Follow these measures to copy in the required formatting and retain it for easy management:

- Take the information from the Word document and copy it.
- Paste the data into the empty Excel spreadsheet (starting with cell |A1|, for example).
- On the ribbon, choose the Data menu.
- Select the text to column key.
- In this conversion column wizard, choose delimited.
- Tick the OTHER box and press enter.
- Click finish or next to complete the task.

13.4.8 EXCEL SHOULD BE TAUGHT NOT TO JUMP TO OUTCOMES.

Excel has a habit of formatting data in ways one would not want. For instance, if one type in 10-11-12 as a barcode, Excel would show it as the date. When you reach 012345, Excel removes the leading zero. Write an apostrophe well before the number to solve the problem. However, Excel can continue to confuse certain fractions (such as 3/16) as dates. If one types this into the cell with the leading apostrophe, it will nearly accurately show (towards the left of the cell, not the right), but if one includes the cell in the calculation, you will get nonsense outcomes.

Adding a leading zero and a gap, like this: 0 3/16, is the answer. One might try pressing Ctrl-Shift-~ to add general formatting to restore the original entry, but they will actually have to rewrite the whole cell.

13.4.9 FORMAT JUST A PORTION OF THE CELL

Pressing the F2 Key and select the portion of the cell one wants to format, or press the formatting shortcut key, including Ctrl-B/ Ctrl-I, or using Format | Cells to add formatting to the chosen section of the cell.

13.4.10 IN EXCEL, INSERT CREDIT CARD NUMBERS

Excel doesn't accept moreover than 15 digits in the cells due to the way it stores data, and when one inserts longer numbers, it normally transforms them or attaches a zero. If you need to list a long string of numbers, such as a credit card no., use an apostrophe before it.

CONCLUSION

Excel is the industry standard for database applications that are often used for money management, financial planning, and data entry. MS Excel, like every other piece of software, isn't flawless. Once you buy a certificate, weigh the benefits and drawbacks to see if Excel is correct for you. MS Excel is commonly used for data collection and organization, which is one of their most basic functions. Information may be conveniently sorted into neat columns and rows, then categorized by kind of data. While a vast array of data in its raw form may be difficult to see, the program's resources enable users to produce displays in which the data is analyzed and inserted into graphs, charts, or tables for easier visualization and analysis. One of the most important features of Excel is the capacity to arrange vast volumes of data into coherent, organized spreadsheets and graphs. It's a lot simpler to interpret and process data when ordered, particularly when used to generate charts and other visual data interpretations.

Excel processes numbers in a fraction of a second, rendering mass calculations much simpler than using a calculator. Formulations and calculations are used to easily compute both basic and complicated equations using vast quantities of data, depending on the knowledge and experience with Excel. This software is available in a variety of formats, including phones and tabs.

Most other spreadsheet applications can import Excel sheets and work on them.

The benefits do not end here; start with Microsoft excel today and learn for yourself.

Made in the USA
Coppell, TX
17 September 2024

37427932R00111